EXPLORING SECOND LANGUAGE READING: ISSUES AND STRATEGIES

KU-072-701

Neil J. Anderson

Brigham Young University

A TeacherSource Book

Donald Freeman
Series Editor

Heinle & Heinle Publishers
I(T)P An International Thomson Publishing Company

Boston • Albany • Bonn • Cincinnati • Detroit • London
Madrid • Melbourne • Mexico City • New York • Pacific Grove
Paris • San Francisco • Tokyo • Toronto • Washington

BLACKBURN COLLEGE
LIBRARY
Acc. No. BB03228
Class No. UCL 428.2407 AND
Date 14|2|06

The publication of *Exploring Second Language Reading: Issues and Strategies*
was directed by members of the Newbury House ESL/EFL
Team at Heinle & Heinle:

Erik Gundersen, Senior Editor, ESL/ELT
Charlotte Sturdy, Marketing Director
Mike Burggren, Production Services Coordinator
Thomas Healy, Developmental Editor
Jill Kinkade, Assistant Editor
Stanley J. Galek, Vice President and Publisher/ESL

Also participating in the publication of this program were:

Designer: Jessica Robison
Production: Su Wilson
Project Management and Composition: Imageset
Manufacturing Coordinator: Mary Beth Hennebury
Associate Market Development Director: Marianne Bartow
Cover Designer: Ha D. Nguyen

Copyright ©1999 by Heinle & Heinle Publishers

All rights reserved. No part of this publication may be reproduced or transmitted in any
form or by any means, electronic, or mechanical, including photocopy, recording, or any
information storage or retrieval system, without permission in writing from the publisher.

Heinle & Heinle is a division of International Thomson Publishing, Inc.

Manufactured in Canada

ISBN 0-8384-6685-0

Dedication

To the many students who have sat through reading classes with me as I have developed my personal philosophy of teaching. Thank you for allowing me to discover how the theory and practice come together for readers.

Thank You

The series editor, authors and publisher would like to thank the following individuals who offered many helpful insights throughout the development of the TeacherSource series.

Jo Ann Aebersold	Eastern Michigan University
Linda Lonon Blanton	University of New Orleans
Tommie Brasel	New Mexico School for the Deaf
Jill Burton	University of South Australia
Margaret B. Cassidy	Brattleboro Union High School, Vermont
Florence Decker	University of Texas at El Paso
Silvia G. Diaz	Dade County Public Schools, Florida
Margo Downey	Boston University
David E. Eskey	University of Southern California
Alvino Fantini	School for International Training
Sandra Fradd	University of Miami
Jerry Gebhard	Indiana University of Pennsylvania
Fred Genesee	University of California at Davis
Stacy Gildenston	Colorado State University
Jeannette Gordon	Illinois Resource Center
Else Hamayan	Illinois Resource Center
Sarah Hudelson	Arizona State University
Joan Jamieson	Northern Arizona University
Elliot L. Judd	University of Illinois at Chicago
Donald N. Larson	Bethel College, Minnesota (Emeritus)
Numa Markee	University of Illinois at Urbana Champaign
Denise E. Murray	San José State University
Meredith Pike-Baky	University of California at Berkeley
Sara L. Sanders	Coastal Carolina University
Lilia Savova	Indiana University of Pennsylvania
Donna Sievers	Garden Grove Unified School District, California
Ruth Spack	Tufts University
Leo van Lier	Monterey Institute of International Studies

TABLE OF CONTENTS

ACKNOWLEDGMENTS

I thank and acknowledge Donald Freeman, the series editor for **TeacherSource.** I believe wholeheartedly in the approach he has taken with this teacher training series. I thank him for his patience with me as I put my philosophy on paper. I have benefited from this reflective process. Donald's input and encouragement have been instrumental. Thanks also go to the editorial team at Heinle & Heinle Publishers. This is my second opportunity to work with the professionals at Heinle & Heinle. I thank Erik Gundersen and Thomas Healy who have been wonderful about keeping this project on schedule. Also, I appreciate the excellent feedback I received from Cherry Campbell and the anonymous reviewers. Their input allowed me to further clarify my thinking.

Especially I want to thank Paul Hardin, Rachel Manning-Smith, Carolyn O'Keefe, and Dawn Turton for their Teachers' Voices. I hold each of these colleagues in the highest esteem. They have been able to allow me, and the readers of this text, to look into their classrooms. They have shared their introspections willingly. It is not an easy task to share what you do as a teacher and to articulate what you think as you develop your philosophy of teaching reading.

I thank Kathy, Cameron, Todd, Amy, Ryan, and Douglas. The support I receive from my family allows me to engage in exciting projects like writing this book.

I do hope that as teachers and teachers-in-training use this text, it may be instrumental in helping them formulate their own philosophy of how to approach the teaching of reading. Ultimately, the best teachers are those who go beyond the recipes and how-to ideas to formulate their own philosophy. I look forward to the continual learning process of discovering how to approach the skill of reading with second language learners.

SERIES EDITOR'S PREFACE

As I was driving just south of White River Junction, the snow had started falling in earnest. The light was flat, although it was mid-morning, making it almost impossible to distinguish the highway in the gray-white swirling snow. I turned on the radio, partly as a distraction and partly to help me concentrate on the road ahead; the announcer was talking about the snow. "The state highway department advises motorists to use extreme caution and to drive with their headlights on to ensure maximum visibility." He went on, his tone shifting slightly, "Ray Burke, the state highway supervisor, just called to say that one of the plows almost hit a car just south of Exit 6 because the person driving hadn't turned on his lights. He really wants people to put their headlights on because it is very tough to see in this stuff." I checked, almost reflexively, to be sure that my headlights were on, as I drove into the churning snow.

How can information serve those who hear or read it in making sense of their own worlds? How can it enable them to reason about what they do and to take appropriate actions based on that reasoning? My experience with the radio in the snow storm illustrates two different ways of providing the same message: the need to use your headlights when you drive in heavy snow. The first offers dispassionate information; the second tells the same content in a personal, compelling story. The first disguises its point of view; the second explicitly grounds the general information in a particular time and place. Each means of giving information has its role, but I believe the second is ultimately more useful in helping people make sense of what they are doing. When I heard Ray Burke's story about the plow, I made sure my headlights were on.

In what is written about teaching, it is rare to find accounts in which the author's experience and point of view are central. A point of view is not simply an opinion; neither is it a whimsical or impressionistic claim. Rather, a point of view lays out what the author thinks and why; to borrow the phrase from writing teacher Natalie Goldberg, "it sets down the bones." The problem is that much of what is available in professional development in language-teacher education concentrates on telling rather than on point of view. The telling is prescriptive, like the radio announcer's first statement. It emphasizes what is important to know and do, what is current in theory and research, and therefore what you—as a practicing teacher—should do. But this telling disguises the teller; it hides the point of view that can enable you to make sense of what is told.

The **TeacherSource** series offers you a point of view on second/foreign language teaching. Each author in this series has had to lay out what she or he believes is central to the topic, and how she or he has come to this understanding. So as a reader, you will find this book has a personality; it is not anonymous. It comes as a story, not as a directive, and it is meant to create a relationship with you rather than assume your attention. As a practitioner, its point of view can help you in your own work by providing a sounding board for your ideas and a metric for your own thinking. It can suggest courses of action and explain why these make sense to the author. And you can take from it what you will, and do with it what you can. This book will not tell you what to think; it is meant to help you make sense of what you do.

The point of view in **TeacherSource** is built out of three strands: **Teachers' Voices**, **Frameworks**, and **Investigations**. Each author draws together these strands uniquely, as suits his or her topic and more crucially his or her point of view. All materials in **TeacherSource** have these three strands. The **Teachers' Voices** are practicing language teachers from various settings who tell about their experience of the topic. The **Frameworks** lay out what the author believes is important to know about his or her topic and its key concepts and issues. These fundamentals define the area of language teaching and learning about which she or he is writing. The **Investigations** are meant to engage you, the reader, in relating the topic to your own teaching, students, and classroom. They are activities which you can do alone or with colleagues, to reflect on teaching and learning and/or try out ideas in practice.

Each strand offers a point of view on the book's topic. The **Teachers' Voices** relate the points of view of various practitioners; the **Frameworks** establish the point of view of the professional community; and the **Investigations** invite you to develop your own point of view, through experience with reference to your setting. Together these strands should serve in making sense of the topic.

Given the importance of reading as a sociocultural skill in modern society, it is not surprising that discussions of how best to teach it have been surrounded by a great deal of theoretical and ideological debate. To a certain extent, however, the teaching of second/foreign language reading, apart from literacy instruction, has escaped the rawness and positioning of these discussions. In his book, *Exploring Second Language Reading: Issues and Strategies,* Neil Anderson approaches teaching reading in second languages from a practitioner's point of view, linking it as a critical step in the chain of academic success. Using a framework organized around the acronym ACTIVE, he argues that teaching reading must combine work on vocabulary and comprehension which draws on learners' prior knowledge, with attention to strategies, reading rate, and motivation. Although Anderson focuses on teaching reading to learners at the adult and secondary levels who are literate in their first languages, the solidness of his approach makes it relevant to other contexts as well. In a field in which contrary positions are common, Anderson writes as a pragmatist. His aim is a personal one: to engage his readers in a process of thinking and development, based on the one he has gone through himself as a reading teacher and one who has studied relevant theory and research. His intention, as he puts it, is "to get readers to think" and thus to develop their own strengths in this vital arena of instruction.

This book, like all elements of the **TeacherSource** series, is intended to serve you in understanding your work as a language teacher. It may lead you to thinking about what you do in different ways and/or to taking specific actions in your teaching. Or it may do neither. But we intend, through the variety of points of view presented in this fashion, to offer you access to choices in teaching that you may not have thought of before and thus to help your teaching make more sense.

— *Donald Freeman, Series Editor*

1

INTRODUCTION TO THE TEACHING STRATEGIES

Reading is an essential skill for English as a second/foreign language (ESL/EFL) students; and for many, reading is the most important skill to master. With strengthened reading skills, ESL/EFL readers will make greater progress and attain greater development in all academic areas.

Reading is an active, fluent process which involves the reader and the reading material in building meaning. Meaning does not reside on the printed page, nor is it only in the head of the reader. A synergy occurs in reading which combines the words on the printed page with the reader's background knowledge and experiences. Readers move through the printed text with specific purposes in mind to accomplish specific goals. In the ESL/EFL reading class, however, one great challenge is that even when students can read in their second language, much of their reading is not fluent. Students are not actively engaged with the text in a meaningful way. They may be moving through it one word at a time and not reaping the joys of reading.

Second language reading teachers face many challenges in the classroom. Teaching students how to utilize the skills and knowledge that they bring from their first language, developing vocabulary skills, improving reading comprehension, improving reading rate, teaching readers how to successfully orchestrate the use of strategies and how to monitor their own improvement are some of the elements that teachers must consider in preparing for an ESL/EFL reading class.

Consider Scarcella and Oxford's (1992) analogy of a tapestry as it relates to the issues of reading. Learning to read is a process, just as learning to weave a tapestry is a process. Various strands of thread are used by the weaver just as various reading skills are used by the reader. It would be rare to find two identical tapestries in the world, just as it would be difficult to find two readers who use identical reading skills and strategies to achieve reading comprehension. Understanding main ideas, making inferences, predicting outcomes, and guessing vocabulary from context are all reading skills that readers of English typically need to develop. Each of these skills is a separate strand of thread used by the reader. Reading strategies utilized by the reader to accomplish these reading skills are also separate threads used by the reader.

In addition to these threads used by readers, there are threads available to reading teachers: the threads of reading theory and pedagogy to develop reading lessons. The threads available to the teacher are also woven into the fabric of the tapestry. The weaving together of all these threads—reading skills, reading strategies, reading theory, and reading pedagogy—creates a tapestry that will be unique to each reader and each teacher in a reading classroom.

In keeping with the philosophy of the **TeacherSource** materials, this text is *not* designed to teach second language instructors how to teach reading. *Exploring Second Language Reading* will present *issues* and *strategies* that teachers can consider. Together we will examine important questions about these issues and strategies. The issues discussed here are appropriate for secondary level ESL/EFL teachers as well as teachers working with adults in higher education or adult education. I will not deal with literacy development issues, but will discuss issues for teaching second language reading to individuals working towards improved reading in English.

Exploring Second Language Reading reflects my personal philosophy of second language reading. It explains how my philosophy has developed over the years and why I have the beliefs I do. It provides opportunities for you to read comments from other ESL/EFL teachers and teachers in training about elements of the philosophy. My intent is not to convince you that my philosophy is the "correct" way to teach second language reading but to get you to think about the process I have gone through and to have you go through a similar process so that you can develop your own strengths as a reading teacher.

Each reading teacher must develop his/her own philosophy for the actual teaching of reading. Perhaps this text will facilitate the development of your philosophy. The development of my own reading philosophy began as I started teaching an ESL reading class. I am sincerely interested in learning more about the theories and models of reading developed by reading researchers. Thus my philosophy began by looking at research related to first and second language reading, and it continues to be influenced by the second language reading research literature and my thinking about how the research findings can be directly applied to my ESL reading classes.

MODELS OF THE READING PROCESS

How do we make sense of printed material? What is involved in reading? How is it that we are able to read? These are questions that I have asked myself as I prepared to teach ESL/EFL reading. I believe that it is important for me to understand this process we call reading so that I can then be better prepared to facilitate the learning of this skill.

Understanding the process of reading has been the focus of much research. Models of how the printed word is understood have emerged from this research (Goodman, 1973, 1976; Gough, 1985; Rumelhart, 1985; Stanovich, 1980). These models can be divided into three categories: bottom-up models, top-down models, and interactive models.

Bottom-up or data-driven models depend primarily on the information presented by the text. That information is processed from letter features to letters to words to meaning. Bottom-up models emphasize what is typically known as "lower-level" reading processes. Segalowitz, Poulsen & Komoda (1991) indicate that these lower-level processes consist of

Bottom-up
models

word recognition and include visual recognition of letter features, letter identification, the generation of grapheme-phoneme correspondences, utilization of orthographic redundancies such as regularities in letter sequences, the association of words to their semantic representations, possibly the identification of basic syntactic structures within the portion of text currently being read, and with the generation of propositional units. (p. 17)

In contrast to bottom-up models, top-down models are diametrically opposed (Stanovich, 1980) to these lower-level processes. Top-down models "all have in common a viewing of the fluent reader as being actively engaged in hypothesis testing as he proceeds through text" (Stanovich, 1980, p. 34). In top-down models "higher-level processes . . . direct the flow of information through lower-level processes" (ibid.). Segalowitz, Poulsen, and Komoda (1991) point out that this

Top-down models

higher level is concerned primarily with integration of textual information and includes resolving ambiguities in the text, linking words with their co-referents, integrating propositional units across sentences, generating and updating a schema or representation of the text as a whole, and integrating textual information with prior knowledge. (p. 17)

The models that are currently accepted as the most comprehensive description of the reading process are interactive models. This third type combines elements of both bottom-up and top-down models assuming "that a pattern is synthesized based on information provided simultaneously from several knowledge sources" (Stanovich, 1980, p. 35). Stanovich states that in interactive models "processes at any level can compensate for deficiencies at any other level. . . . Higher processes can actually compensate for deficiencies in lower-level processes" (p. 36). Murtagh (1989) stresses that the best second language readers are those who can "efficiently integrate" both bottom-up and top-down processes (p. 102).

Interactive models

Grabe (1991) emphasizes two conceptions of interactive approaches. The first relates to the interaction that occurs between the reader and the text. This suggests that meaning does not simply reside in the text itself but that as readers interact with the text their own background knowledge facilitates the task of comprehending. The second conception of interactive approaches relates to the interaction between bottom-up and top-down processes. Fluent reading involves both decoding and interpretation skills. With the research completed to date on reading processes in both first and second language reading we know that reading integrates several skills, strategies, and processes and is not a simple event to describe. Grabe points out the complexity of even defining reading by stating that "a description of reading has to account for the notions that fluent reading is rapid, purposeful, interactive, comprehending, flexible, and gradually developing" (p. 378).

As I have observed my students in the reading class and reflected on these three models which try to explain the reading process, I can see that an interactive model is the best description of what happens when we read. Second language readers do some bottom-up things when they read (decode unfamiliar vocabulary, struggle with poor print quality of a handout I have given them, wonder about a part of speech of a particular word), and they do some top-down things when they read (anticipate what is coming next in the text, draw on their previous experience). I believe my teaching of reading has improved as I have come to understand that reading is an interactive process of both bottom-up and top-down models.

STRATEGIES FOR CONSIDERATION IN TEACHING SECOND LANGUAGE READING

This text addresses the integration of theory and practice through eight teaching strategies for second language reading classes. This framework developed as I struggled as a teacher to develop my own voice from the pages of research and suggestions by others that I have read. I wanted to be able to integrate several key ideas I had learned from the research of others into a pedagogical framework that would help guide me in my teaching. I wanted to be able to find a word that I could use to remind me of key elements of my personal philosophy of reading. The word I chose was ACTIVE. I like this word because it not only helps me remember six elements of my personal philosophy, but it also reminds me that reading is an active process and not a passive skill.

For more on the ACTIVE framework see N.J. Anderson, 1994

The word ACTIVE introduces the first six strategies I would like us to consider when teaching an ESL/EFL reading class:

A Activate prior knowledge

C Cultivate vocabulary

T Teach for comprehension

I Increase reading rate

V Verify reading strategies

E Evaluate progress

The remaining two strategies deal with the role of motivation and planning and selecting appropriate reading materials.

Although looking at these issues in linear form makes it appear that there is a sequence to the philosophy in its application to teaching, this guiding frame is not to be viewed as sequential but very interactive. Each of these issues overlaps with others. References to related ideas throughout the text will be made to help the reader see the interconnectedness of the strategies. Recall the image of a tapestry. One thread in the tapestry does not create a pattern in the cloth. It takes several strands of thread overlapping and interacting with all the other strands to create the beautiful pattern. This emphasizes the interactive nature of the reading process, that each skill and strategy ties into others.

I do not want to suggest that the eight strategies addressed in this book are the only elements to consider when preparing your own personal philosophy for teaching reading. However, these eight have been central to my philosophy.

Each strategy will be addressed from three aspects: **Teachers' Voices,** **Frameworks,** and **Investigations.** The **Teachers' Voices** will allow us to hear from ESL/EFL reading teachers regarding the teaching strategies addressed in the text. Four teachers/teachers-in-training have agreed to share their perspectives on the teaching strategies discussed. I will also be sharing my voice with you; I begin each chapter with an experience from my own life that I have found has influenced my thinking about teaching and learning.

Dawn Turton is a Graduate Teaching Assistant in an intensive English program at a Midwestern university where she is enrolled in the MA Linguistics program. She has taught EFL for 4 years in Greece, Korea, Poland, and Taiwan. She has plans to begin a Ph.D. program in Applied Linguistics and desires to be a TESL/TEFL teacher trainer. Dawn's thinking about these reading strategies can best be classified as coming from an *inservice* perspective. Teaching reading is not new for her. She continues to gain insights into her own teaching as she reflects upon helping her students increase their reading skills. My interaction with Dawn came in various forms: interviews, e-mail, and chats in the hallway at the university.

The Teachers' Voices

Rachel Manning-Smith is a graduate student in an MA program. She is a "typical" *preservice* teacher. Rachel did not have any ESL teaching experience upon entering the MA program. The ideas and concepts presented are very much in a "theoretical stage" for her. She thinks about reading from her own experience and wonders how these teaching strategies will work with ESL/EFL learners.

Carolyn O'Keeffe works with ESL teachers and Instructional Assistants in the Northshore School District in Bothwell, Washington, as the District Pre-K–12 ESL Coordinator. She also works with preservice teachers and teachers with certification at the University of Washington ESL education courses. She has worked for 19 years as an ESOL professional.

Paul Hardin is the ESL Coordinator at the Clover Park School District in Lakewood, Washington. He has worked for 22 years as a public school teacher and has taught grades K–12. He has coordinated the K–12 program for the district for 18 years. He is currently teaching full time at the high school level.

These four teachers will provide insights into how these teaching strategies have worked for them. This text provides the unique opportunity to hear these teachers' voices clearly.

Another section in each chapter is the **Frameworks.** Here I share with you aspects of second language reading theory that have influenced my teaching philosophy. Each of the strategies that are addressed has some data that can help to shape our thinking about how to approach the development of a reading curriculum and lesson planning.

Finally, the **Investigations** section provides opportunities for you as reader/ teacher to reflect upon and experiment with some of the teaching strategies discussed. These investigations are designed to get you thinking about and refining your own philosophy about how to teach reading. I remind you that it is not important that we agree on the implementation of these eight teaching strategies, but that we each have a philosophy about how reading can be taught to second language readers and that we are each able to articulate what that philosophy is.

1 *Make a notebook for yourself to use during your reading of this book. We will refer to this as your Reflective Reading Journal. A three-ring binder might work best because you can add to and remove paper from it without major difficulties. Divide the notebook into eight sections, one for each of the teaching strategies we are going to address:*

Strategy 1: Activate Background Knowledge

Strategy 2: Cultivate Vocabulary

Strategy 3: Teach for Comprehension

Strategy 4: Increase Reading Rate

Strategy 5: Verify Reading Strategies

Strategy 6: Evaluate Progress

Strategy 7: Build Motivation

Strategy 8: Select Appropriate Reading Materials

There will be **Investigations** opportunities for you to reflect back on earlier entries you have made in your Reflective Reading Journal. When you finish you will be able to piece together your thinking from this journal into your own personal philosophy on how to teach second language reading.

2 *Think about the eight teaching strategies to be addressed in this book. (Review the list in Investigation 1 above.) Is there one of these teaching strategies that you would consider more important that any of the others? Why? Record your ideas in your Reflective Reading Journal.*

3 *Respond to the following questions in your Reflective Reading Journal.*

1. Define reading in a second language.

2. Do you enjoy reading in your native language?   yes no

3. How long do you read daily (on average) in your native language?

4. What types of materials do you read in your native language?

5. Do you enjoy reading in your second language? Why? Why not?

6. How long do you read daily (on average) in your second language?

7. What types of materials do you read in your second language?

8. List five things you consider strengths about your reading in your first language.

9. List five things you consider strengths about your reading in your second language.

10. What overlap do you see in your responses to questions 8 and 9?

11. List five things you would like to improve in your first language reading.

12. List five things you would like to improve in your second language reading.

13. What overlap do you see in your responses to questions 11 and 12?

14. What is the title of your favorite book?

15. What is your favorite movie?

16. What is your favorite type of music?

17. What are some of your hobbies?

18. For questions 14-17 above, do you find yourself reading material that deals with any of these topics? Why? Why not?

19. Do you know someone you would say is a good reader?

20. What makes this person a good reader?

21. Do you know someone you would say is a poor reader?

22. What makes this person a poor reader?

23. What do you hope to learn by reading this text on teaching strategies for the second language reading class?

CONCLUDING THOUGHTS

The process of preparing this book has reinvigorated me and my thinking about the second language reading process. My Reflective Reading Journal is full of ideas I want to talk with other reading teachers about and experiment with in my classroom. My hope is that you too will become excited about engaging in a discussion of the teaching strategies to be discussed and that you will experiment with and reflect upon these strategies for the improvement of language instruction.

2

STRATEGY ONE

ACTIVATE PRIOR KNOWLEDGE

1 *How do you believe that prior knowledge influences the reading process of second language readers? What have you observed or experienced that has led you to this belief? Record your thoughts in your Reflective Reading Journal.*

2 *What role does background knowledge play in our understanding of texts? Record your ideas in your Reflective Reading Journal.*

> *Passage 1:* John knew his wife's operation would be expensive. There was always Uncle Harry. John reached for the suburban telephone book.

Reflective Questions: Is Uncle Harry related to John or John's wife? How close is John to Uncle Harry? How do you know that? Is Uncle Harry a medical doctor? Is Uncle Harry rich?

> *Passage 2:* Jane was invited to Jack's birthday party. She wondered if he would like a kite. She went to her room and shook her piggy bank. It made no sound.

Reflective Questions: How old is Jane? How old is Jack? What leads you to your answer? What sound did Jane expect to hear when she shook her piggy bank? What if the piggy bank is filled with currency and not coins?

> *Passage 3:* Mary heard the ice cream man coming down the street. She remembered her birthday money and rushed into the house . . . and locked the door.

Reflective Questions: How old is Mary? What leads you to your answer? Why would she go into the house and lock the door? Do you think she is "protecting" her money from her younger brother who likes to buy ice cream?

> *Passage 4:* Mary heard the ice cream man coming down the street. She remembered her gun and rushed into the house.

Reflective Questions: How old is Mary? What leads you to your answer? Why would she think of her gun when she heard the ice cream man?

Passage 5: The tubes were barreling. He was stoked, so he waxed his machine. As he paddled into the line-up, a set was lined up to the horizon. He took off on the third one, pulled off a 90 bottom turn and hit the lip, did a fly-away cut-back into the soup, pulled backed into the tube and barreled for a solid five. He kicked out 200 yards down the beach.

Reflective Questions: What is happening in this passage? What is a tube? How do tubes barrel? What is the lip? What is the soup?

Passage 6: The innings opened briskly. Mr. Barrow, who was rather a showy bat, though temperamental, took the bowling at the factory end of the pitch and cheered the spirits of his side by producing twos in the first over. Mr. Garrett, canny and cautious, stonewalled perseveringly through five balls of the following over and then cut the leather through the slips for a useful three. (From Dorothy Sayers', Murder must advertise, 1967, p. 250).

Reflective Questions: What is happening in this passage? What is a first over? What is the leather that is cut through the slips? What is a useful three?

Each of the six passages in Investigation 2 above is culturally biased. Which ones were you able to read and understand without major problems? Which ones caused you difficulty?

I have problems with passages 5 and 6. I am not very familiar with the sport of surfing (passage 5) or the sport of cricket (passage 6). It is difficult for me to retell what I have read from these passages because I lack the background knowledge and experience playing or watching these sports. The vocabulary seems very strange to me. I read these passages frequently to remind myself that the students in my reading classes may be experiencing the very same thing when I ask them to read about topics that are new to them.

One of my hobbies is gardening. I enjoy getting out into the dirt. The smell of freshly turned soil appeals to me. I enjoy mowing the lawn. Some consider these tasks tiresome and boring. There is a certain degree of satisfaction that I enjoy upon completion of the work. As I sit on my deck on a Saturday afternoon when the flower beds have been weeded and the soil turned and the grass mowed I get a certain sense of satisfaction that does not come any other way.

My wife and I grow a vegetable garden. During most of our married life I have taken responsibility for tilling the garden bed and getting the soil ready for planting and Kathy has done the actual gardening. We also have flower beds and several house plants. I guess we've divided the labor. I take care of the flower beds and indoor plants and she takes care of the vegetable garden.

For many years I have taken great care of plants. I have recently taken greater care in mixing my own soil (and not simply using the soil straight from the bag from the store). I read about the type of soil mix the houseplant needs and then follow the instructions to develop the growing "foundation" that the plant needs, and make sure that the right amount of water and sunlight is given, which is vital to the growth of the plant. I have always had great "luck" with

African violets. The plants in my office are healthy and strong with almost continual blooms throughout the year.

Recently I built compost bins. I dump leaves, grass clippings, sawdust, food scraps, anything organic, into the bins and stir it all up. In order for the materials to decay quickly I need to turn the compost over regularly so that oxygen can get to the center of the decomposing materials and facilitate the process of breaking down the organic material.

As I have reflected on my success with the flower beds at home, with the house and office plants, and with the vegetable garden, I recognize that this success is directly related to the time and care invested early in the gardening process. The preparation prior to planting has been a key to success in this hobby.

The same is true of reading. A certain amount of time and work is needed prior to engaging in a reading passage. Teaching a second language reader how to approach a text in order to get the most out of it is a teaching strategy that needs to be developed and improved by second language teachers.

Just as plants need different types of soil for best growth, teachers need to provide variety in the activities used in the classroom for activating the prior knowledge of the readers.

Second language learners are much like plants. They require constant attention to make sure they are getting the right amounts of the ingredients that will help them grow and improve as learners.

When asked about activation of background knowledge a group of teachers responded with the following:

- our background knowledge is like a lens through which we understand what we read

- activation of background knowledge allows the teachers to unlock vocabulary before reading

- SQ3R (survey, question, read, recite, review) is an activation of background knowledge strategy that many textbooks suggest that students use. I wonder if learners really use this activation technique on their own when the teacher is not there to remind them to use it?

- Part of our goal in the reading class should be to make our readers independent. Teaching them how to draw upon their background knowledge is one way to make readers independent.

Teachers' Voices

The role of prior knowledge and reading

A reader's background knowledge can influence reading comprehension skills. Background knowledge includes all experience that a reader brings to a text: life experiences, educational experiences, knowledge of how texts can be organized rhetorically, knowledge of how one's first language works, knowledge of how the second language works, and cultural background and knowledge, to name a few areas. Background knowledge is also referred to as schema in the reading literature (schemata for plural).

Frameworks

For more on
schema theory
see Carrell,
1983a; 1983b;
and 1984

A significant amount of research has been conducted by second language reading researchers indicating that reading comprehension and reading skills are enhanced when prior knowledge is activated. Adequate data suggest that "inducing appropriate schemata through suitable pre-reading activities is likely to be extremely beneficial" (Murtagh, 1989, p. 102). The notion of prior knowledge influencing reading comprehension suggests that meaning does not rest solely in the printed word, but that the reader brings certain knowledge to the reading that influences comprehension. Carrell and Eisterhold (1983) point out that "a reader's failure to activate an appropriate schema . . . during reading results in various degrees of noncomprehension" (p. 560). Thus, activation of prior knowledge facilitates comprehension. In addition, research on knowledge of text structure indicates that the reader's understanding of how texts are organized influences reading comprehension. Carrell and Connor's (1991) research examines ESL readers' abilities to read descriptive, persuasive, and narrative texts. Their findings support the idea that knowledge of text structure influences reading comprehension.

For more
on schema
theory and text
structure see
Carrell, 1984
and 1985

McNeil (1987) suggests that activation of background knowledge can be initiated by setting goals, asking questions, and making predictions. He indicates that

> [e]fficient readers approach reading tasks in a more active, strategic, and flexible fashion than poor readers. Poor readers' passivity is reflected in their lack of predicting and monitoring activities: They do not pose questions, identify a goal, or check the extent to which answers have been confirmed. (p. 49)

Some readers may not have prior knowledge to activate. For example, as we saw in passages 5 and 6 of Investigation 2, readers may not have previous experience of playing certain sports. If you have no knowledge of how the sport is played, or the vocabulary involved in it, you have no background knowledge to activate prior to reading about it. In such a case, it will be necessary for the reading teacher to establish background prior to asking the students to read so that they have sufficient information to understand the text.

An interesting concept to consider related to the role of background knowledge is the negative influence it may have. Can background knowledge hinder comprehension? For example, some readers may have misconceptions about how AIDS is contracted. Some may believe that you can get AIDS by kissing, swimming in a pool, shaking hands, or donating blood. If students have these beliefs, their background knowledge may interfere with reading. The teacher may have to correct the background knowledge through a pre-reading activity before reading comprehension can be achieved.

3 *You might consider using a semantic mapping activity in a reading class you are teaching now. Before conducting the activity, carry out the activity yourself. Choose a topic of an upcoming reading passage and create your own semantic map. Share your map with a colleague and discuss the use of this technique in a reading class. (For a discussion of semantic mapping, see page 14.)*

4 *Think of a reading passage that you have covered that was very new to the readers. What could you do to build some background knowledge prior to asking the students to read the passage? Record your ideas in your Reflective Reading Journal.*

R ead as Carolyn O'Keeffe, from the Northshore School District in Bothell, Washington, describes a few of the activities she does to activate the background knowledge of the secondary school ESL readers that she teaches.

A fun activity that I've suggested and teachers have used to activate background knowledge in literature is the following. Students listen as the teacher describes the story: setting and scenery, theme, and major characters. Students add input as they feel comfortable on what they know about such a setting, theme and/or the characters. They are then given a large piece of construction paper (14 x 24) and are instructed to draw and color a map of the story scenes. They don't add the action. Once they've done this, they turn to a partner and describe and share what they drew and why. On separate circles, they draw each main character as they "see" them. Again, they share their drawings with a partner. The students enjoy this activity. It makes the literature selection more vivid for them, and they are using another intelligence by drawing and coloring. As they read the story and discuss in class (whole group and partners), the teacher instructs them to choose the major actions of the story and draw and color each one on a separate circle. These circles can be sequenced, placed within the map, and/or categorized in a chart by which person performed the action. Before they draw the actions in each circle, the students share their choices with their partners. A whole class discussion can occur after the partner sharing. Students are asked to "defend" their choices.

Another activity that I have used with academic reading is the use of pictures. On the overhead projector, I write three columns: What We Know, What We Predict, and What We Found Out. Students write the same columns in their notebooks. I have them look at the pictures and other graphics within the chapter we are about to read. The students then discuss what they discovered with a partner and then we discuss it as a whole class. They write down what we "know" about the chapter in the first column. Next, I have students read the first paragraph and share what they learned with their partner. From these discussions, I ask them to predict what they think the chapter will be about. Again, they share this with their partner before we do a whole class share. After our class discussion, the students write down what they predict the chapter's content will be. As students read the chapter, they can add to the third column information that they found out.

5 *If you could talk to a reading researcher about studies conducted on the role of background knowledge in L2 reading, what would you ask? Write one question. Be specific. Write that question in your Reflective Reading Journal.*

If you have access to an ESL/EFL reading researcher, ask your question. Remember that many researchers are accessible on e-mail and enjoy engaging in discussion about reading theory and application of that theory to the classroom. Try contacting someone via e-mail. Then, record your thoughts and what you have learned from this exchange in your Reflective Reading Journal.

6 *Has research on the role of background knowledge influenced your teaching? How? Record your thoughts in your Reflective Reading Journal.*

Frameworks

Possible classroom activities to activate prior knowledge

Several classroom activities can be prepared to facilitate the activation of prior knowledge. First, pre-reading discussions provide an opportunity for readers to see what they know about a topic and what others may know. This discussion can best be directed by the teacher asking questions about the topic. An idea for managing a pre-reading discussion is suggested by Dubin and Bycina (1991). They recommend the use of what they call "anticipated guides" which contain "a series of statements, often provocative in nature, which are intended to challenge students' knowledge and beliefs about the content of the passage" (p. 202). This is a particularly useful classroom activity because sometimes students may not realize that they have prior knowledge on a particular subject, but as they listen to other students share information, they come to realize that they indeed know something about the reading topic.

Second, a pre-reading discussion on the type of text structure and what expectations a reader may have about the organization of the material is very valuable for ESL readers. This could include a discussion of the kinds of transition or linking words that the reader can expect to find. See page 47 for a list of common transition words which may prove useful.

Consider what you might do to establish background knowledge of students in your class. One technique that I have seen used in the public schools is the use of Language Experience Approach (LEA). LEA allows all members of the class to experience an activity together; that activity then becomes the basis for language and content instruction. This is an excellent way to integrate the teaching of language and content. (Content-based instruction will be explored in Teaching Strategy 3: Teaching for Comprehension.) Also, LEA allows for a natural context to integrate the teaching of reading and writing.

Semantic mapping

Another way to build or establish background knowledge that may be lacking in the students you work with is through the use of semantic maps. Semantic mapping is similar to brainstorming. The readers may be given a key word or concept that will be part of the reading material. They are then asked to generate words and concepts they associate with the key word. The material can be graphically organized on the chalkboard. Semantic mapping allows students to link ideas and concepts they already know to the new concept that will be learned, thus helping to build background knowledge prior to reading. For example, if you were going to introduce a reading passage to a group of high school ESL learners about Acquired Immunodeficiency Syndrome (AIDS) you could conduct a semantic mapping activity to determine the current background knowledge of the class. Begin with the word AIDS written in the center of the chalkboard and ask students to share key vocabulary and concepts about AIDS that they are aware of. Your map might look something like the one below:

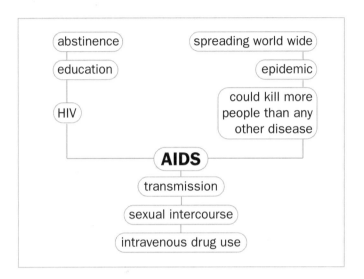

A very useful web site that has proven to be helpful to me can be found at the following URL:

http://www.ncrel.org/sdrs/areas/issues/students/learning/lr1grorg.htm

Go to this web site and see some of the examples it gives for graphic organizers.

Activation of prior knowledge of text organization can facilitate reading comprehension. If readers understand possible ways that a cause and effect text could be organized, the knowledge can help them understand that kind of text. Knowledge of how arguments are presented in writing can help readers move through a text more efficiently. Lack of knowledge of the rhetorical pattern would not present a reading comprehension barrier for the reader, however.

Next, if readers will make predictions about what they think the text content will be, they can then read to support or reject their hypotheses. This particular activation activity would need to be tied into activities that are used during later phases of the reading lesson, particularly an activity to verify whether the predictions that were made prior to reading were actually realized in the reading passage. Recall how Carolyn reported using this activity in her high school ESL class.

A final idea is to have students monitor their use of background knowledge activation strategies as they read outside of structured classroom activities. Conduct a class discussion on a regular basis and ask the students what kinds of things they do to activate their background knowledge when they are reading something that has not been assigned for school work. It would be helpful for you also to share with the students what you do to prepare to read.

Dawn is teaching a reading class in an intensive English program with students who are also enrolled in one academic course at the university. She has been thinking about many of the concepts discussed above. Together we have discussed what techniques teachers can use to activate students' background knowledge prior to undertaking a reading task. Let's look at what Dawn has been experimenting with.

I worked quite a bit this past week on activating background knowledge. I tried some different things. When my students do homework I always get them to write down a list of strategies they've used. I have them write down some ideas that the title has generated or what they know. My students make notes about what they already know about the topic. I have them reading things from their own disciplines. I also have them exchange ideas from their own disciplines after they make notes.

I had an African Studies major give a reading to someone who was in Sports Science. And the Sports Science major read something from the African Studies major. They each didn't think they would know much about the other's area of study. The Sports Science major said he didn't know much about Africa. So I asked him to write down what he does know about African business. He said that there wasn't much business in Africa. I asked him why he thought that, and he said because it was a poor continent and the people didn't have much to eat so how can there be much business. Many things that he thought about Africa came up in what he wrote. He mentioned Africa's dependence on the West, selling raw materials to the West and then buying them back.

I thought back on the principle of activating the student's background, about activating what they do know and letting the students know they do know something. Everybody knows a little bit about things that they read. It's very rare that I've done something in class that nobody knows anything about.

I also did another reading this week entitled, "Does civilization owe a debt to beer?" I wrote the title on the board and asked what they thought it meant. Initially they said they didn't know anything. I asked them to think what it could possibly mean. I put them in small groups and they had to generate an idea. They came up with some really good ideas. One group thought it was an analogy because they thought that civilizations take a long time to develop . . . and good beer takes time to develop. So they had this analogy going. Another group came up with the idea that civilizations develop only when you have schools and education and you need to raise taxes. So the only way you could raise taxes was by having a tax on alcohol. So the reason that we have a good school system is because so many people drink beer in the U.S. and the government gets all of the taxes. Then a third group thought about how language developed. When beer was "discovered it made people more sociable and thus language developed." So they generated a lot of ideas just from the title.

I then had them scan the article and determine whose idea most closely fit what they learned from scanning.

I worry that when they are reading at home they don't even look at the title, that they just start reading. I ask them what they are doing. Are they actually using these strategies to activate their background knowledge? They know what I'm asking for in class, but I wonder if they really do this at home? Do they even look at the title? Some of them have said that they find it helpful.

Some of my students have said that they make questions based on the title and scanning the passage and then they are more motivated to read to find the answers.

I had a TOEFL reading passage the other day in class on positive and negative electric charges. One student hears the word science and says that he's a business major and thinks he will not understand anything. So some of these techniques help me to get them into the passage. It keeps students motivated, particularly the graduate students.

I read an idea on activation of background knowledge from Dubin and Bycina. They make a statement about the use of provocative statements. We read an article about English only. We discussed which language we should pick if there could be only one language. This provocative statement gets them thinking. If I ask them, "what do you think about this?" I really get no response, so a provocative statement gets them thinking, especially at 4 o'clock in the afternoon. I told them that because I was British I thought we should all speak British English. They sat there and processed what I said and they started talking and generating ideas.

I also believe that these are helpful techniques because the students are relying more on each other. They are generating ideas in groups. I find that once students leave the intensive English program they don't go to see their professors. If they are having problems with the reading they just sort of panic. They realize that their classmates can help them. If you don't know anything about African culture you can talk with someone who may know more about it. Many of the students are in similar classes once they leave the intensive English program. I know they are still reluctant to talk to American students. But they know they can talk to other people in the class.

This is tied to vocabulary. I ask students to generate vocabulary, to "write down 20 words you think will occur in the text." Then I ask them to sort their lists by verbs and adjectives. At least they are activating what they expect to find.

7 *Talk with someone currently teaching reading and ask whether/how he/she activates background knowledge prior to introducing a reading passage.*

8 *How do background knowledge activation techniques vary according to the type of passage the students are reading? For example, how would your techniques for activating background knowledge differ when preparing students to read a textbook chapter versus reading a newspaper report on the weather forecast? What kinds of things could you do to prepare students to read poetry? Record your ideas in your Reflective Reading Journal.*

9 *Review an ESL/EFL reading text for examples of activation of background knowledge. How do textbook authors activate readers' background knowledge? What supplementary activities could you propose? Discuss your findings with a colleague.*

10 *If you are teaching a reading class, try out some of these ideas and write a short reaction piece on what happened.*

11 *If you have access to the World Wide Web, go to the TESL-L archives and do a search of the previous discussions that have taken place among ESL/EFL teachers around the globe on the activation of background knowledge. What do you learn about activation of background knowledge from reviewing these e-mail exchanges? Record your ideas and thoughts in your Reflective Reading Journal.*

To become a member of the TESL-L discussion group (which will not only give you access to the complete archives, but also the chance to participate in on-line discussions and to join the TESL-L special interest branches) do the following: Send an e-mail message to LISTSERV@cunyvm.cuny.edu. The subject line should be left blank. The text of the message should be sub tesl-l first name last name. For example, if I were subscribing my message would be: sub tesl-l neil anderson.

12 *Does your experience in teaching reading support or reject these ideas about the role of background knowledge in reading? You do not have to agree with these ideas, but it is important that you think through what you do believe about the role of background knowledge in reading and why.*

CONCLUDING THOUGHTS

Reflect back on the analogy of gardening I used earlier. What I do while gardening relates so very well to language teaching. I prepare compost to be mixed with the garden soil. This can be related to building background knowledge for our readers which some may be missing. The soil must be rich in order to allow the seed to prosper. The better the preparation of the soil the better the results of the garden. When I take time to turn the soil, get rid of weeds and prepare a fertile growing environment, the garden prospers. So it is with our learners in the reading class. If we take the time to prepare them, sometimes having to fill in for missing or weak background knowledge, the rewards later are tremendous.

Carolyn and Dawn have shared with us some of the techniques they use in their reading classes. Involving students in art projects prior to reading as well as during the reading process allows for different types of learners to have needs met. Making predictions based on a passage title also seems effective.

Based on what we have learned from second language reading research, activation of prior knowledge can influence reading comprehension. Perhaps reviewing some of this literature will provide you with additional reasons for considering this factor in your personal philosophy of teaching reading.

Suggested Readings

Patricia Carrell has done more work on the role of background knowledge and second language readers than any other scholar that I am aware of. Two key articles which anyone really interested in this topic should review are two of the first she wrote on the topic, both published in 1983. Look in the References at the end of this book for Carrell, 1983a; 1983b. These articles will provide a view of the role of background knowledge which has only been strengthened with additional years of research. An article she wrote in 1985, also listed in the References, is useful in getting a perspective on the influence of text structure on reading comprehension.

Richard Pritchard published an insightful article entitled "The Effects of Cultural Schemata on Reading Processing Strategies" (1990) which is an excellent example of research that examines the role of background knowledge and how reading is influenced.

Richard-Amato's *Making It Happen: Interaction in the Second Language Classroom* (1996) provides a brief but useful discussion of anticipation guides along with other pre-reading activities.

Each of these suggestions can provide input into the development of your philosophy of the value of activating background knowledge prior to reading.

3

STRATEGY TWO
CULTIVATE VOCABULARY

I have been running for approximately 20 years. During this period there have been some intense times and some lax times. I remember reading a running book when I first started running and the author stated that a real commitment to running requires that you keep running and not just do it for a short period of time.

I have participated in four marathons. Twenty-six point two miles is a long way. Before each marathon I spent time reading on the best preparation techniques. I set a training schedule so that I could mark my progress and growth. I knew that I needed to gradually add miles to my schedule. I couldn't run the full 26.2 miles all at once but each week of training I ran farther until I was confident I could run the full distance.

The key with the training runs for me was to have some long runs followed by short runs the next day. I usually had one run a week that would be longer than the runs the rest of the week. I found this to be very effective. Again, I didn't try to get in shape all at once.

For three of the marathons I trained by myself and ran the day of the race as a loner. The last marathon I ran I trained and ran with a friend. I found that it was helpful to have someone to run with. This cemented my commitment. I knew that I had to get up early on those Saturday mornings to go for a long run because someone else was counting on my being there.

Even as I write this material now, I am preparing to run a half-marathon with a few friends. I integrate my running with other exercise. I try to spend two days each week lifting weights to provide some variety to the exercise routine. Also, I have recently added cycling to the routine. I find that having more than one way to achieve my goal of being physically fit is important in preventing exercise burnout.

My running has really just been a hobby. I'm not fast and have never come close to being at the front of the run. But, I have kept on running and have made it a regular part of my exercise routine.

The acquisition of vocabulary is much like my training runs. Readers cannot develop all their vocabulary skills overnight. The vocabulary workouts need to be part of an overall reading improvement program. Knowing a lot of words does not mean that you can read. Adding a regular, steady study of vocabulary to your reading improvement can provide consistent development and growth toward your goal of increasing your knowledge of words and how they work.

Vocabulary doesn't develop overnight

1 *Refer back to Investigation 3 in Chapter 1,* Introduction to the Teaching Strategies *(page 6). Did your definition of second language reading include a statement about knowing vocabulary? What do you think that says about your personal philosophy on teaching reading? Record your ideas in your Reflective Reading Journal.*

2 *Refer back to Chapter 1, Investigation 3. Look at questions 21 and 22. Does* the poor *reader you know have weak vocabulary skills? What about the* good *reader discussed in questions 19 and 20? Record your ideas in your Reflective Reading Journal.*

Let's read now what Paul thinks about the role that vocabulary instruction plays in second language reading.

> I feel vocabulary development is one of the most critical areas of second language reading. Vocabulary is the fuel that ignites the fire of reading and comprehending what one reads (William Grabe, personal communication). This becomes very clear as I watch my students reading narrative stories and see many students meticulously looking up every word they don't understand in a bilingual dictionary, while others, more interested in completing the exercise in class and not having homework, push on trying to get meaning out of the text by using pictures and guessing what the author is attempting to communicate. The advocates of the bilingual dictionaries feel they are not learning if they don't look up every word and try to discern some meaning from the text, while the other students feel it is a waste of time to look up every word when they know they may never see it again and besides, "I can figure out the story without knowing the word." I take these two extreme opposite student views on vocabulary development and choose strategies that will assist the adamant user of the bilingual dictionary to rely less on that strategy and the perpetual guessers to be a little more educated in their approximations of vocabulary and text meaning. This method is shared with the students. They are aware of the technique and how the strategies will provide them with skills and not just learning a list of words. They will be able to leave their reading and use those skills in Math, Science, and any other class they are taking. To assist them in seeing this as reality, I use textbooks from the students' science, math and history classes to demonstrate how the strategy can be applied across all curricular areas. This provides purpose and motivation to students to develop increased vocabulary awareness.
>
> To cultivate vocabulary in L2 reading, I look at the abilities seen in good L1 readers as they relate to vocabulary and its role in the

reading process. Some of these include but are not limited to: the ability to recognize word parts such as prefixes, word stems, etc.; the ability to recognize parts of speech and how they relate to word meaning; fluent and automatic word recognition; a large recognition vocabulary; the ability to project meaning by using clues within the context; and a knowledge of how the world works.

One of the strategies I use as teacher is to have a print-rich environment with posters and charts on the walls with words and phrases on them. I have books, magazines, phone books, menus, flyers, newspapers, cookbooks, and other reading materials around the room to encourage the students to read extensively.

The major concern my students have, appearing through each period of the day, is "I don't understand the words in the book, so I can't do the work." As a starting point for increasing recognition vocabulary I explain to my students that the most successful way to acquire a larger vocabulary is through extensive reading. This includes reading during class time as well as after school and weekends, reading beyond the required homework assignments, and reading for fun as well as for information. To facilitate this task I have my students make personal dictionaries related to class assignments and word lists related to additional personal reading.

At the beginning of a lesson the students will examine the cover or title page of a book and brainstorm the type of vocabulary that may be in the story they are about to read. The students will then create a semantic map and attempt to group or categorize the words into related concepts. This is done as a whole group and gives the students success with the story from the beginning because they realize how much they already know about the reading just from the first page. This gives me a better understanding of their background knowledge in this particular area. I can tell if the students are familiar with the possible story line or the topic of the reading. I do this for both narrative and academic reading. This also gives me a baseline of vocabulary with which students as a group are comfortable.

To further the students' success with the story the class works together to help those who are not familiar with some of the words on the semantic map. Then we talk about word usage and what the jobs of those words might be in the story we are about to read. This allows a discussion of parts of speech and how they can further our understanding of the text. These exercises warm up the students and decrease the anxiety level of dealing with new material, especially a reading from the field of biology or any other academic area. I become a participant in this phase of the lesson. I also provide words to the semantic map. I try to choose words that will be part of the focus vocabulary for the lesson. It may not be obvious to the students at first, but it becomes understandable when I ask them to explain the relationship of the words to the theme of the reading.

The next activity would be the first reading of the text to confirm or adjust the student's predictions. This reading is done silently. Once the discussion of the predictions is completed, the students place any focus words into their personal dictionary. I usually have no more than ten words that are focus words or words crucial to understanding the text. The personal dictionary is a graphic organizer that has a column for:

Word	Page	Sentence from reading	Definition	Your Sentence
			(*your words*)	

All other words are placed on the student's Word List. These "throw-away words" are used in other activities related to this story or other stories. Words from "extensive reading" after school are also added to this word list. Since it is the student's learning list, they can put whatever information they need. Some students put a definition, some students put an equivalent term in their first language, and some students use it in their own sentence.

One activity I use to build recognition and fluency and to use the throw-away words is Word Recognition Exercises. In these exercises I include focus vocabulary, throw-away words, and high frequency words. The inclusion of high frequency words helps build a stronger foundation for those readers who have limited L1 literacy. The activity lists the key word in the first column followed by four distracters or words that look similar to the key word plus the key word again in a random position among them:

walk   walks   walked   talked   walk   wall

The students are given 40 seconds to find and circle the key word in the group of distracters. This exercise can be used to practice focus and throw-away vocabulary, troublesome spelling words, phonics, morphological changes, synonyms and antonyms, prefixes, suffixes and word stems. The number of items can be increased as the exercise is repeated to increase recognition and fluency to reading.

These are some of the activities I use to help my students develop strategies to learn and comprehend vocabulary. Many of my students are able to "read" anything they are given. They have the ability to name (sound out) words and this causes confusion in other classes. Teachers see that they can "read" the words and then assume the second language readers understand the words or have the skills to use a dictionary or "figure out" the meaning. Most of the time the students have no comprehension of the words they "read." They are simply naming words. I stress the importance of understanding key words using the above strategies and putting less emphasis on secondary or less important words. Use your time to comprehend, to read extensively and vocabulary building will take place as result of increased reading.

The role that vocabulary plays in the reading process continues to be an area of research in second language learning. Many second language readers cite "lack of adequate vocabulary . . . as one of the obstacles to text comprehension" (Levine and Reves, 1990, p. 37). Grabe (1991) stresses the important role of vocabulary as a predictor of overall reading ability. Nation (1990) emphasizes "a systematic and principled approach to vocabulary by both the teacher and the learners" (p. 1) and says that in order for instruction to be effective the teacher needs to make informed decisions about how to teach vocabulary. He suggests five reasons why a concentrated focus on cultivating vocabulary is needed. (1) Research findings suggest a great deal "about what to do about vocabulary and about what vocabulary to focus on" (p. 1). (2) A variety of ways are available to classroom teachers for presenting needed vocabulary. Teachers might consider how they will address vocabulary instruction and not ignore it simply because they do not like one particular method for teaching vocabulary acquisition. (3) Researchers and students alike "see vocabulary as being a very important, if not the most important, element in language learning" (p. 2). (4) Readability research suggests that vocabulary plays a crucial role in development of reading skills as well as academic achievement. (5) "Giving attention to vocabulary is unavoidable" (p. 2). Independent of the language teaching methodology employed in the language classroom, second/foreign language teachers might consider if and how vocabulary instruction will be addressed in their classroom. Discovering for yourself how you will approach the teaching of vocabulary is a part of your teaching philosophy which requires careful thought and reflection.

As I have developed my own philosophy of the role of vocabulary in reading instruction, I have decided that basic vocabulary should be explicitly taught and L2 readers should be taught to use context to effectively guess the meanings of less frequent vocabulary. I have arrived at my philosophy in part by reviewing the research on vocabulary acquisition. Levine and Reves (1990) have found in their research that "it is easier for the reader of academic texts to cope with special terminology than with general vocabulary" (p. 37). They stress the great need for a teaching program which builds general, basic vocabulary. McNeil (1984) recommends that vocabulary learning techniques "emphasize concern for active processing of new vocabulary so that vocabulary development enhances reading comprehension, not just word knowledge" (p. 123).

Perhaps the most important theoretical consideration in vocabulary instruction is summarized in these three questions from Nation (1990):

1. What vocabulary do my learners need to know?

2. How will they learn this vocabulary?

3. How can I best test to see what they need to know and what they now know? (p. 4)

With these questions in mind, effective vocabulary instruction can be achieved.

The role of vocabulary and reading

For more on vocabulary research see Cohen, 1987; Huckin, Haynes, and Coady, 1993; and Nation, 1990

Questions a teacher can consider to determine vocabulary instruction

These theoretical threads lead naturally into the possible classroom applications. Nation (1990) recommends that language teachers "make a distinction between direct and indirect vocabulary learning" (p. 2). To do this, he provides four ways that vocabulary instruction can be integrated into language learning. These four principles are listed "from most indirect to the most direct" way to teach vocabulary. (1) Explicit preparation of language learning materials through carefully controlling the vocabulary presented in written texts. (2) Discussion of unfamiliar vocabulary as it naturally comes up. Nation indicates that this is perhaps the most common method of vocabulary instruction. (3) Teaching vocabulary in connection with other language activities. For example, Nation suggests that prior to reading a passage or listening to a text, learners could be provided with essential vocabulary. Vocabulary exercises may also follow language activities. The thrust of Nation's suggestion is that the vocabulary is learned as part of another language activity. As mentioned earlier, this also serves the function of activating the prior knowledge of a reader. (4) Teaching vocabulary independent of other language activities. Actual classroom activities that typically fall into this classification of vocabulary instruction include: knowing spelling rules, analyzing word structure, mnemonic techniques, paraphrasing activities, and vocabulary puzzles.

Possible classroom activities to cultivate vocabulary

Nation (1990) and Cohen (1987) outline similar methods of assisting second language learners in acquiring new vocabulary. Four techniques they discuss include: rote repetition, use of context, mnemonic approaches, and analysis of word structure.

Rote memorization

Rote memorization and repetition suggest that some learners make use of continual repetition of a word and its meaning until they feel the word is learned. The use of flashcards may be a helpful tool for some learners that benefit from this study technique. I would recommend some caution though. Students may spend more time making the flash cards than actually studying the cards.

Using context to guess vocabulary words

Guessing words in context is perhaps the most common vocabulary acquisition skill suggested by reading texts and reading teachers. Clarke and Nation (cited in Nation, 1990) suggest five specific steps which could be included during explicit instruction of this strategy. I would challenge teachers to consider if these steps are an appropriate way to teach guessing vocabulary from context to their students and how they could adapt these steps for their particular teaching situation.

Step 1. Look at the unknown word and decide its part of speech. Is it a noun, a verb, an adjective, or an adverb?

Step 2. Look at the clause or sentence containing the unknown word. If the unknown word is a noun, what adjectives describe it? What verb is it near? That is, what does this noun do, and what is done to it? If the unknown word is a verb, what nouns does it go with? Is it modified by an adverb? If it is an adjective, what noun does it go with? If it is an adverb, what verb is it modifying?

Step 3. Look at the relationship between the clause or sentence containing the unknown word and other sentences or paragraphs. Sometimes this relationship will be signaled by a conjunction like "but," "because," "if," "when," or by an adverb like "however" or "as a result." Often there will be no signal. The possible types of relationship include cause and effect, contrast, inclusion, time, exemplification, and summary. . . . Punctuation may also serve as a clue. Semicolons often signal a list of inclusion relationships; dashes may signal restatement. Reference words like "this," "that," and "such" also provide useful information.

Step 4. Use the knowledge you have gained from Steps 1-3 to guess the meaning of the word.

Step 5. Check that your guess is correct.

    a. See that the part of speech of your guess is the same as the part of speech of the unknown word. If it is not the same, then something is wrong with your guess.

    b. Replace the unknown word with your guess. If the sentence makes sense, your guess is probably correct.

    c. Break the unknown word into its prefix, root, suffix, if possible. If the meanings of the prefix and root correspond to your guess, good. If not, look at your guess again, but do not change anything if you feel reasonably certain about your guess using the context.

    [d.] Using the dictionary could be [an additional] way of checking. (pp. 162–63)

These steps provide a beginning for teachers to consider how to explicitly teach readers how to use context to guess unfamiliar vocabulary.

Using mnemonic techniques has proven to be a widely used approach for remembering new vocabulary. This techniques involves the learner creating an unusual mental image that links the new word with a similar sounding word from the first language. The example that Nation gives is of an Indonesian learner of English learning the word *parrot*. The Indonesian word "parit" meaning "ditch" sounds similar to the English word "parrot." The learner creates a mental image of a parrot in a ditch. The more unusual the mental image, the easier it is for the learner to recall the image and thus the meaning of the new vocabulary word.

> Mnemonic techniques for vocabulary acquisition
>
> For more on mnemonic techniques see Cohen, 1987; and Pressley, Levin and Miller, 1982

Word structure analysis skills encourage the learner to study prefixes, roots, and suffixes and use this knowledge to learn new vocabulary. Nation (1990) states that in order for learners to make use of word analysis, three skills are needed: (1) Recognizing the parts of a word. This is best accomplished by asking learners to break words into their parts. (2) Learning the meaning of prefixes and roots. Simple memorization of the meanings of key prefixes and roots is recommended. (3) Using prefixes and roots. Learners need to be able to combine prefixes and roots to create words and recognize how the combined meanings create the meaning of a word.

> Word analysis skills

Knowing the meaning of prefixes, suffixes, and roots can be a strategy to guessing the meaning of unfamiliar vocabulary. Below is a list of 14 key words that use combinations of prefixes and roots. Knowing these 14 key words can lead to knowing the meaning to over 14,000 words in English (Nation, 1990).

THE FOURTEEN WORDS

Words	Prefix	Common Meaning	Root	Common Meaning
1. precept	pre-	before	cept	take, seize
2. detain	de-	away, down	ten, tain	hold, have
3. intermittent	inter-	between, among	mis, mit	send
4. offer	ob-	against	fer	bear, carry
5. insist	in-	into	sist	stand
6. monograph	mono-	alone, one	graph	write
7. epilogue	epi-	upon	logue	say, study of
8. aspect	ad-	to, toward	spect	see
9. uncomplicated	un- com-	not together, with	plicate	fold
10. nonextended	non- ex-	not out, beyond	tend	stretch
11. reproduction	re- pro-	back, again forward, for	duc, duce, duct	lead
12. indisposed	in- dis-	not apart, not	pose	put, place
13. oversufficient	over- sub-	above under	ficient	make, do
14. mistranscribe	mis- trans-	wrong across, beyond	scrip, script, scribe	write

Investigations

3 *If you are currently teaching an ESL/EFL reading class, give this list of 14 key words to the students and ask them to memorize the list. Find reading passages that contain words with these prefixes and roots in them, thus allowing the students to see how knowing the meaning of the prefix and root can unlock vocabulary power in their reading.*

4 *Select an ESL/EFL reading text. Review a number of the readings in the text to see how frequently the prefixes and roots from the list of 14 key words appear. What value do you see in teaching this list to your students? Record your ideas in your Reflective Reading Journal.*

Teachers' Voices

Listen as Paul describes how he teaches students to use the context to guess the meanings of unfamiliar words they encounter while reading.

Looking around the unknown word and trying to understand its role in that sentence is another strategy I feel is important to vocabulary development. For this activity I examine three techniques used frequently in narratives and academic texts. These are introduced during direct instruction with the whole class. Often I will role-play the strategy by reading a sentence or group of sentences and "thinking out loud" go through the steps of the strategy to determine the meaning of the unknown word, "guess" the meaning or decide that the word is not crucial to understand the sentence, and move on. This is also an activity I have my students do in groups and then for the whole class. This allows extensive practice with the strategy and provides more exposure to all the class. I have found that this strategy works well for such techniques as definition or restatement, synonyms and antonyms. These examples are from a Puerto Rican legend, Lazy Peter and His Three-Cornered Hat:

Lazy Peter *disposed of,* got rid of, three bags of money.

Seeing the bag of money was such a surprise the farmer stood with his mouth open in *astonishment.*

The farmer offered a thousand *pesos,* Spanish coins, for the hat.

In the first example I would role play the steps in the strategy. I would first look at the word and try to determine its role or function in the sentence. It comes after Lazy Peter so it could be a verb. It ends in "ed" or "d." There doesn't seem to be any other verb in the sentence. I think it is probably the verb of the sentence and therefore a key word to understanding the meaning of the sentence. Are there any other clues around the word? The next three words are set off by a comma. "Got rid of," could be the meaning of "disposed." Does it make any sense if I use it instead of "disposed?" Lazy Peter got rid of the three bags of money. Yes, "disposed of" must mean "got rid of." As students increase their exposure to these techniques the process becomes more automatic.

In the second example, the role play would be similar to the first. The first part of the sentence up to the comma is understandable. The next part has the "farmer stood with his mouth open," that is still understandable. The last part, the farmer was surprised, standing with his mouth opened in surprise, so astonishment must mean the same as surprise.

In the third example, I know "thousand is an adjective so pesos must be a noun, and plural because thousand means more than one." "Offered" is the verb, but he offered what? It must be pesos, so that word is important to understanding the sentence. I see the next words are in commas. That must have the meaning in it.

One additional area of vocabulary research which I have found interesting and helpful is the use of frequency lists. There are approximately 2,000 words that account for almost 80% of the words found in average texts (Coady et al., 1993). Given that we know about these highly frequent words, teachers might consider how they can teach readers to recognize them automatically.

Frequency lists

For more on
frequency lists
see Coady et al.,
1993; and
Nation, 1990

Coady et al. (1993) suggest that because these words occur so frequently there is justification for significant commitments of instructional or learning time. They suggest that direct instruction of vocabulary is best done by treating the vocabulary word in context.

Rachel asks some very interesting questions about word analysis skills development and second language readers. Recall that Rachel does not have any teaching experience so these are questions that cross her mind as she considers the application of this idea.

> I personally believe that cultivating the vocabulary is the most important thing.

> Let's take word analysis skills for example. I'm just very curious because there have to be cases where students have analyzed a word and they get the wrong meaning. And they go on thinking they know what this word is and they really don't and it's going to cause problems. They might not realize they have the incorrect meaning until they come across the word again in another text. They may not realize they have the wrong meaning while reading this text.

> Let's take the prefix in-. In some cases it means "not" in others it means "in" or "into."

> What about words like insect?

> Students need to be taught that the letters in- at the beginning of a word do not necessarily mean that the prefix is being used.

> How do students know when it is a prefix and when it is not? It looks like it could be.

> I assume that it is through my education and my exposure to many texts that I know this.

> I know for a fact that no one ever told me you can't do this with the word insect. So how is it that I know? Somehow I just learned that "in-" in this word is not a prefix. It is probably because I already knew what insect meant.

> If students came across the word insect and they've never seen the word and they decide that they can analyze the word and they see "in-" they may guess not and "sect" is a suffix which means section or divide. They would arrive at a meaning of not divided. How are they going to know that this is not the meaning of insect?

> I guess that ties into evaluation of the strategy of word analysis. At some point they are going to know that the way they have applied the strategy of word analysis for this word was not correct. I think I'm beginning to see.

Rachel might have added that even if students interpreted the "in-" in "insect" as meaning "in" or "into," thus arriving at "cut into" or "divided into" (the actual derivation of the word, referring to insects' segmented bodies), they would still be unlikely to make the jump from this to "insect." In fact "in" *is* a prefix in "insect"—but not a useful one for getting the meaning.

Paul has experienced the teaching of prefixes and suffixes with the secondary level students he is working with. He tells us . . .

> Another difficulty students experience is the addition of prefixes and suffixes to words with which they are already familiar. Students will have on their Word List examples such as *unfortunate, misunderstood, graceful, unhappy,* etc. I ask them to look into the word and see if they recognize another word. They will look at "unhappy" and see "happy" and explain that they understand "happy" but not "unhappy." Many times they are unable to find such words in their bilingual dictionary or English dictionary. We talk about the word stem "happy" and what happens to it when "un" is added to the beginning. They recall the prefix and its negative connotation. Awareness of word stems, prefixes, and suffixes is discussed as a vocabulary development strategy. The students work through exercises as a class and individually. They work with these concepts in relation to a context, never in isolation. The transfer is not always at the point of direct instruction. It may be a reading three days later where "misunderstood" appears and the student hits a road block. "I don't know the word. It's not in my bilingual dictionary. It's not in my English dictionary. I can't understand the story." At that point I begin to recycle the lesson of three days ago and ask the student to look inside the word and find all the words he/she recognizes. At times I will role-model that activity for the student and I'll look inside the word and work through the strategy with the student. I will identify "understood" and then look at the beginning "mis." I will begin to think back to that lesson and look at "mis" as something added to the word stem "understood" to change the meaning. Usually by this time the student will have picked up on this and remembered the meaning of "mis" as a prefix. Students begin to see that what they did three days ago as a "lesson" can be used in a "real story" or in their science book. They begin to realize the role of extensive reading and practice. It didn't happen three days ago during the lesson, but today when one student was at an end point and could move no further, the recycled strategy helped that student see the connection between affixes and word meaning.

Paul Nation has prepared a computer program, *Vocab Profile,* which allows a teacher to compare the text of a reading passage against a vocabulary frequency list. The program is designed only for DOS computers. *Vocab Profile* allows you to see what percentage of the vocabulary in a text is at various levels of difficulty. The program can also be used to compare the vocabulary of two (or more) texts to see how much of the same vocabulary is used in both passages and where the vocabulary differs.

Computer applications and software

At the time of publication of this text the web address where *Vocab Profile* can be downloaded is

http://www.stir.ac.uk/epd/celt/staff/higdox/listers.htm#nation.

5 *If you have access to the World Wide Web, download Nation's* Vocab Profile *and run it on a reading passage you are using. What do you learn about the level of vocabulary difficulty from this exercise?*

Computer software

Auseful piece of software designed for Macintosh computers is *NewLexis.* This program is for individual study of frequent vocabulary; it allows a reader to learn vocabulary in context. The software provides practice opportunities in five ways: (1) matching words to definitions, (2) matching definitions to words, (3) completing sentences with missing words, (4) spelling missing words, and (5) spelling defined words. The vocabulary words have been divided into sets of 100 words, with 64 sets currently available. The vocabulary is tied to Nation and Magoto's (n.d.) *University Word List.* Words range in difficulty from beginning level vocabulary to advanced.

Concordancers

One additional way in which the computer can be a very valuable resource for vocabulary instruction is through concordancing. Concordancers were once thought to be tools used only by researchers, but now they are a useful tool for language teachers. One concordancer *MonoConc* is available on the Web at http://www.athel.com/mono.html.

A concordancer allows a reading teacher to examine the lexical, syntactic, and semantic patterns in several reading passages. For example, if you had four reading passages on the topic of AIDS that you were going to introduce to your class, you could use *MonoConc* to examine the word frequencies of the vocabulary. The concordancer can facilitate the identification of high frequency vocabulary in the reading materials you plan to use. It is an effective tool which reading teachers often are not aware of.

6 *Write Hyperbole Software for a demonstration copy of* NewLexis. *At the time of publication of this book the address is 5 Sunnyside Drive, Athens, OH 45701-1919 USA. Telephone: (614) 594-4609. Try out the software. How would this form of vocabulary study be beneficial to your students? Ask your students to experiment with the demonstration copy. What are their reactions to this form of vocabulary study?*

7 *If you have access to the Web, download the concordancing program* MonoConc. *Apply it to a text you are using for a reading class. What do you learn from this process?*

8 *Review an ESL/EFL reading text for examples of vocabulary instruction. How does the text cultivate the acquisition of vocabulary? Do you believe that the approach will achieve its purpose? How might you supplement the text with more expansive vocabulary work?*

9 *Talk with someone currently teaching a reading class and ask whether/how he/she cultivates vocabulary.*

10 *If you are teaching a reading class, consider which of the approaches to vocabulary instruction might work best given your students' needs, then try out some of the approaches to vocabulary instruction we have discussed. Write a short reaction piece about what happened. What did you do? Do you think that the activation activity achieved your objective? Record your ideas in your Reflective Reading Journal.*

The Internet is an excellent resource available to teachers. I have found the following Web sites of interest in the development of vocabulary skills.

Internet
Resources

http://www.aitech.ac.jp/~teslj/cw

This site has crossword puzzles which are very good for vocabulary development.

http://grove.ufl.edu/~tsniad/

The ESL Vocabulary Construction site brings together resources, online exercises, and activities.

http://www.swan.ac.uk/cals/bibl/varga97.html

This site is an archive of research papers and resources. If you substitute 96 for 97 you will find the resources published in 1996; 95 for 97 gives you resources published in 1995. The list includes years 1991 through 1997.

http://www.eslcafe.com

Dave Sperling's ESL Cafe includes more than just vocabulary activities. Lesson plans, games, and resources are available.

http://www.swan.ac.uk/cals/vlibrary/pm96d.html

A virtual library of the Vocabulary Acquisition Research Group at the University of Wales headed by Paul Meard.

11 *If you have Internet access find each of the five sites listed above. Record in your Reflective Reading Journal what you found valuable from these sites. How can the activities on these sites help improve the way you cultivate vocabulary skills?*

The use
of authentic
materials for
vocabulary
instruction

Authenticity of reading material is a subject that some teachers discuss with their colleagues. We all want to be able to use *real* materials in our reading classes which the students will encounter in the *real* world of reading. These *real* materials provide a rich source for vocabulary instruction.

For the intermediate and advanced proficiency levels, finding authentic materials is not very difficult. Ask the students what they like to read and what they have to read. Use those materials in class.

For beginning proficiency level classes, the use of authentic materials is more challenging. Finding material that is appropriate for teenage and adult readers can present an obstacle for many teachers. I have found that for this level of language proficiency I have to adapt materials to meet the reading levels of my students. I then make sure that I engage the students in an authentic reading activity with the adapted materials that I have prepared. Teachers could benefit from considering the authentic use of the reading material and not being overly concerned that they cannot find authentic materials for their beginning level students.

12 *Find an authentic reading passage. Review the vocabulary and determine an appropriate way to cultivate the vocabulary skills of potential readers.*

Rachel has come across an interesting insight which highlights how the elements of ACTIVE reading are integrated and cannot be examined in isolation. Read about her analysis of the relationship between cultivating vocabulary and increasing reading rate (to be discussed in more detail in Teaching Strategy 4: Increase Reading Rate.)

> These vocabulary study strategies have an impact on a student's reading rate. Let's say that you get to a word and you decide that you need to dissect it so you have to stop to analyze the word; then you read on and you get to another word, and then you use the context to guess the meaning. The student ends up reading slowly.

> I do see a relationship with the reading strategy of SQ3R (survey, question, read, recite, review). Vocabulary study doesn't occur during the reading phase of SQ3R. It would come during survey, question, or review. Interesting.

Vocabulary
acquisition and
learning style

One final area I would like to present for your consideration is how learning style may influence the cultivation of vocabulary. We know from learning style research conducted by Joy Reid (1995) that some students prefer to learn alone while others prefer to learn in groups. The individual/group learning style preference is a variable which might be of interest to you in the development of philosophy of cultivating vocabulary in the reading class. I try to allow for both individual and group activities when using any of the instructional strategies discussed here. Students who prefer to work in groups can often learn more vocabulary when studying with others than by working alone.

Levine and Reves (1990) point out that in vocabulary teaching "frequent and numerous recycling should be . . . emphasized" (p. 45). All students do not learn vocabulary in the same way, nor do all vocabulary words lend themselves to one method of acquisition. Levine and Reves support this idea by advising that teachers not "impose any one specific method on the learner. Vocabulary should be presented by a variety of techniques: methods should be varied and combined according to the learner's individual needs and preferences" (p. 45). Words that lend themselves to a structural analysis can most appropriately be learned through the use of the structure technique. Other words may more appropriately be learned through the use of a mnemonic keyword approach.

A great deal of overlap exists between development of vocabulary skills and the teacher's ability to select appropriate materials for the reading class. Strategy 8: Plan for Instruction and Select Appropriate Materials includes some ideas for consideration that relate to vocabulary level.

CONCLUDING THOUGHTS

Four ideas from my running experience have helped me to formulate my personal philosophy of reading. First, running is a long term commitment, not just a fad. Teachers might consider how the cultivation of vocabulary skills will be addressed within a reading program. I would advocate that it not simply be a fad. Second, when I have trained for a marathon I've had to gradually increase my mileage so that I would be prepared for the full 26.2 mile run. Vocabulary study could be integrated throughout the reading process and not something that is done all at once. Next, sometimes I have run alone and on other occasions I have run with a friend. Using both of these study strategies may be helpful for second language readers who are developing vocabulary skills. Studying alone at times is a very appropriate strategy. Remember that studying with a friend or group of friends may also be beneficial. Finally, running is a regular part of my exercise routine. It is part of my goal to be physically fit. Additional types of exercise add variety so that I don't suffer from running burnout. Vocabulary study may be viewed as a regular part of reading instruction. It is part of a larger context, not an activity that is done in isolation from other reading skills and strategies. I have continued to enjoy running after all of these years. It has become part of what I see myself continuing to do for some time ahead. Likewise, vocabulary study may be viewed as a skill that second language readers see as being part of their study of language today and in the future.

Suggested Readings

Three books provide valuable insights into the role of vocabulary and second language reading. For a more in-depth treatment of this component of the reading process you should consult these resources. First, Evelyn Hatch and Cheryl Brown (1995) won the annual Mildenberger prize in 1996 for the book that significantly contributes to the teaching and learning of second and foreign languages, *Vocabulary, Semantics, and Language Education.* They include an excellent section with three chapters on lexical cases and morphology. Also of special notice in this book is the section on vocabulary learning and teaching.

Second, Tom Huckin, Margot Haynes, and Jim Coady (1993) have published a valuable book entitled *Second Language Reading and Vocabulary Learning*. Three chapters of greatest interest to the role of vocabulary and language teaching include: "High Frequency Vocabulary and Reading Proficiency in ESL Readers" (Coady, Magoto, Hubbard, Graney, and Mokhtari), "Procedural and Declarative Knowledge in Vocabulary Learning: Communication and the Language Learners' Lexicon" (Robinson), and "Factors Affecting the Acquisition of Vocabulary: Frequency and Saliency of Words" (Brown).

Finally, *Teaching and Learning Vocabulary* by I. S. P. Nation (1990) has influenced my thinking on how to teach vocabulary to second language readers. In addition to the 12 chapters which provide excellent insights, Nation includes in Appendix 2 a university word list of frequent vocabulary for second language readers in university contexts. The list provides a frequency rating of key vocabulary used in such contexts.

These books will provide valuable input in helping you refine your personal teaching philosophy of the role of vocabulary and second language reading.

4

STRATEGY THREE

TEACH FOR COMPREHENSION

In recent years I have become interested in the art of bonsai. The process of aging a young tree is very interesting. What I have found most fascinating is that you can train a young tree in its growth and development so that it looks strong and mature even though it is small and delicate.

My first attempt with this new hobby was to order two small trees from a mail order catalog. I was so excited when the packages arrived. I was so disappointed when I opened the box and found such a small plant. It didn't look anything like the picture in the catalog or in the books I had been reading. I followed the directions from a book I had been reading. I anchored the roots in the small pot. I clipped and pruned the branches to give shape to this little plant. I wrapped wire around the branches to train them to grow in the direction I wanted. I watered and tended the little trees.

I began to wonder if I was pushing the little tree into maturity too quickly. I had clipped its roots, wired the branches, and forced it into a small pot within a very short time. Was I trying to move through the maturing stages too quickly?

Unfortunately, our family took a vacation shortly after this project was started. We had invited a neighbor to water the house plants. When we returned I realized that the bonsai didn't look very healthy. Eventually I had to discard the little trees.

Now, you would think that this would discourage me. I continued to read and learn more about the art of bonsai. I talked with a TESOL colleague who is also interested in bonsai. Just listening to her talk about her delight in this hobby increased my interest.

I decided that another way to get into this emerging interest was to purchase a tree that was already well trained and to tend and nurture it for a period and learn in smaller stages. This way I would not be trying to do too many things at the same time. This tree is doing very well. I find that each day I devote some attention to it, making sure that new growth doesn't dominate the direction that I see the tree is going, carefully evaluating the amount of water it needs, and regularly spraying it to protect it from disease. Every day the bonsai requires some attention.

I am enjoying this process of carefully examining the tree to determine how to best let it show its beauty and strength.

The art of bonsai is helping me to see the role of teaching reading comprehension skills. My personal teaching philosophy includes this essential component of teaching students how to comprehend. In the early days of developing my philosophy, the T in ACTIVE reading was a reminder to TEST for comprehension. I was sharing this perspective with a group of teachers in South Africa and one very astute teacher asked a simple question, "Neil, we often know how to test a reader's comprehension skills, but how do we teach readers how to comprehend?" What a powerful idea! So powerful that right then and there I changed the T to *teach for comprehension*.

Testing versus teaching reading comprehension

In many reading instruction programs, a greater amount of emphasis and time may be placed on *testing* reading comprehension than on *teaching* readers how to comprehend. Monitoring comprehension is essential to successful reading. Part of that monitoring process includes verifying that predictions that are being made are correct and checking that the reader is making the necessary adjustments when meaning is not obtained. Activation of background knowledge (discussed earlier) is essential to the reading comprehension process. Eskey (1986) states that "comprehension is always directed and controlled by the needs and purposes of an individual and crucially depends on that individual's . . . background knowledge" (p. 6). He further states that "reading comprehension is most likely to occur when students are reading what they want to read, or at least what they see some good reason to read" (p. 6).

Models of reading comprehension

As I have read the literature on issues related to comprehension, two areas have influenced my thinking. First, the development of models of the reading comprehension process and second, the role of metacognitive awareness during reading.

Cognition can be defined as thinking. Metacognition can be defined as thinking about one's thinking. In order to teach for comprehension, it is my belief that readers must monitor their comprehension processes and be able to discuss with the teacher and/or fellow readers what strategies are being implemented to comprehend.

The research (discussed in Chapter 1, Introduction to Teaching Strategies) related to theoretical models of reading comprehension can influence one's thinking about teaching comprehension skills to second language readers. A top-down theory suggests that comprehension is facilitated when a reader's background knowledge is activated. Eskey (1986) indicates that

> [b]oth the general notion of reading as the reconstruction of meaning based on a skillful sampling of the text, and such specific notions as the use of linguistic redundancy, the crucial role of prior knowledge (or nonvisual information) in prediction, and the necessity for reading at a reasonable rate in larger, more meaningful chunks of text are pure Goodman/Smith and now generally accepted ideas about reading. Among second language teachers interested in reading, the top-down model has already achieved something like official status as the model. (p. 12)

Note the importance of larger units of meaning influencing the top-down philosophy of comprehension.

A bottom-up theory suggests the idea that readers build meaning as they draw on the individual letters and words as they read. Eskey (1986) points out that

[t]his model assumes that a reader proceeds (as most readers think they do) by moving his eyes from left to right across the page, first taking in letters, combining these to form words, then combining the words to form the phrases, clauses, and sentences of the text. (p. 11)

Note the sequencing of items in this list, moving from the smallest unit to larger units, thus bottom-up.

An interactive model supports the idea that good readers use both processes, top-down and bottom-up, when they encounter text in order to comprehend. Grabe (1991) illustrates this ...

> [   ]nation
> fı   ıation from
> th   se that many
> sk   378)

University Centre Library
The Hub at Blackburn College

Customer ID: ******54

Title: An introduction to child language development.. [Learning about language.]
ID: BB05383
Due: 20110706

Title: Exploring second language reading : issues and strategies. [TeacherSource]
ID: BB03228
Due: 20110706

Total items: 2
08/06/2011 20:24

Please retain this receipt for your records
Contact Tel. 01254 292165

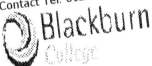

In ter   ents to comprehend
what the   n a reading task we
expect to   nticipating reading
compreh   nguage readers, the
reading p   omprehension will
result, th   y will do in their
classes to

A secor   about the role of
compreher   of metacognitive
skills. This   and will also be
discussed ir   egies later in this
book. Rese   nducted strategy
training exp   . Grabe (1991)
points out t   because of the
promise it ho

Meaning   when the reader integrates   iding, reading
strategies, and   ess by teaching learners h   sider is to get
readers to mo   ely aware of
what they are   y able to discuss how they

R achel has m   uld be used
  in teaching   ot and idea
and is able to g   classroom.
Let's read what   nding as a
teacher-in-trainin

> I like this id[e]   t
> you have to   a
> relatively ne[w]

For more on strategy training experiments see Brown, Palincsar, and Armbruster, 1984; Carrell 1985; Carrell, Pharis, and Liberto, 1989; Palincsar and Brown, 1984; Robinson, Faraone, Hittleman, and Unruh, 1990

Metacognitive awareness

Teachers' Voices

take risks as well and get out of the "old" ways and try some of this newer stuff. It makes sense to me to teach comprehension instead of just test it.

I've thought about how teaching reading comprehension is ideal when students are reading what they want to read. This is ideal, right? Students don't always have the luxury of reading what they want to read. I don't always read what I want to read. Some things you're asked to read may not be really interesting. But it is still important to understand what you have read. It's not always a positive reason. It seems that especially for ESL students reading could be so overwhelming that they're not always enjoying everything they are reading. But they still need to learn how to comprehend.

Sometimes readers think they're understanding when they're not. That's one of the things that I don't like about guessing. Because you guess and you think you're right and all along you're not. How do you teach students to recognize that their guesses are not right? How do you teach them to comprehend?

I like the idea of getting readers to formulate their own questions. But what if the students come up with good questions and then the text doesn't answer the questions? You have to be sure to have good texts. Also, teachers can ask readers what is not comprehended. Sometimes I'm reading and I say to myself that I'm just not getting this but I don't stop to ask myself, what is it that I don't understand? Is it this word? Is it this whole topic? What is it exactly? So this seems like a very simple concept, ask them what they're not understanding. It's a simple thing to do, but it's probably not something I would think to do.

Getting students to paraphrase and summarize is a good way to teach comprehension skills also. I don't know why I keep thinking about this, but I'm just curious if this is a new concept for students. When you say to students to look for the main idea, do they know what to do? Do they have to be taught where the main ideas are in written texts in English?

---

1 *Observe a reading class. Watch for things the teacher does to teach students how to comprehend the text. What is the balance of teaching to testing activities? Record your ideas in your Reflective Reading Journal.*

---

2 *Talk to a reading teacher about teaching learners how to comprehend. What techniques does the teacher suggest for fostering the development of reading comprehension skills? What can you take from this conversation to help you formulate your own philosophy of the role of comprehension in your teaching?*

---

3 *In your own second language reading, monitor your comprehension. What do you do as you read material in your second language? Record your strategies in your Reflective Reading Journal.*

One helpful resource for secondary level ESL teachers in teaching reading comprehension skills is the *ESL Standards for Pre-K–12 Students* developed by the professional organization of Teachers of English to Speakers of Other Languages (1997). The standards movement in public school education is not limited to ESL. Many organizations have developed standards in school subject areas (e.g., The American Council on the Teaching of Foreign Languages, The National Council of Teachers of English with The International Reading Association, The National Council of Teachers of Mathematics, The National Council for the Social Studies).

ESL Standards for Pre-K–12 Students

The ESL standards for grades 9–12 include appropriate standards to include in our discussion of teaching reading comprehension. Goal 2 of the *Standards* relates to preparing students to "achieve academically in all content areas" (Teachers of English to Speakers of Other Languages, p. 127). Two standards related to this goal involve the kinds of reading skills and strategies that ESL/EFL teachers could consider. Standard 2 states: "Students will use English to obtain, process, construct, and provide subject matter information in spoken and written form" (p. 127). The following reading comprehension skills are specifically discussed in the descriptors for this standard:

- listening to, speaking, reading, and writing about subject matter information

- selecting, connecting, and explaining information

- analyzing, synthesizing, and inferring from information

- hypothesizing and predicting

- formulating and asking questions

- understanding and producing technical vocabulary and text features according to content areas

Standard 3 states: "Students will use appropriate learning strategies to construct and apply academic knowledge" (Teachers of English to Speakers of Other Languages, p. 135). The descriptors include the following strategies appropriate for teaching reading comprehension:

- applying basic reading comprehension skills such as skimming, scanning, previewing, and reviewing text

- using context to construct meaning

- applying self-monitoring and self-corrective strategies to build and expand a knowledge base

- planning how and when to use cognitive strategies and applying them appropriately to a learning task

- evaluating one's own success in a completed learning task

Notice the overlap with the standard descriptors above and what we have already suggested for teaching reading comprehension. Although the term *metacognition* is not used above, many of the standard descriptors relate to metacognitive activities: selecting, connecting, and explaining information; formulating and asking questions; applying self-monitoring and self-corrective strategies to build and expand a knowledge base; evaluating one's own success in a completed learning task. Notice the link with concepts we have discussed in previous chapters: understanding and producing technical vocabulary and text features, previewing and reviewing text, and using context to construct meaning.

4 *How could the* ESL Standards for Pre-K–12 Students *assist you in teaching reading comprehension skills rather than simply testing them? Record your ideas in your Reflective Reading Journal.*

Intensive and Extensive reading

An additional area for consideration related to teaching comprehension skills is the relationship between intensive reading and extensive reading. Intensive reading can be defined as using a text for maximal development of comprehension skills. All activities are designed to explicitly teach readers the comprehension skills necessary for them to transfer the strategies and skills to their own reading when they are not in the classroom. Aebersold and Field (1997) emphasize that this type of reading treats the text as the end in and of itself. Extensive reading can be defined as reading large amounts of text for general comprehension. Typically, extensive reading is combined with other activities so that reading is only a portion of what the learner is expected to do. For example, readers may read large amounts of text and then prepare a paper comparing and contrasting various viewpoints on the topic. Or they might use the information read to prepare a persuasive speech to convince someone to agree with their position. Aebersold and Field tell us that this type of reading is a means towards the end.

Day and Bamford (1998) describe ten characteristics of successful extensive reading programs. They suggest that programs with these characteristics allow second language readers to make great progress in the development of reading skills.

1. *Students read as much as possible,* perhaps in and definitely out of the classroom.

2. *A variety of materials on a wide range of topics is available* so as to encourage reading for different reasons in different ways.

3. *Students select what they want to read* and have the freedom to stop reading material that fails to interest them.

4. *The purposes of reading are usually related to pleasure, information, and general understanding.* These purposes are determined by the nature of the material and the interests of the student.

5. *Reading is its own reward.* There are few or no follow-up exercises after reading.

6. *Reading materials are well within the linguistic competence of the students* in terms of vocabulary and grammar. Dictionaries are rarely used while reading because the constant stopping to look up words makes fluent reading difficult.

7. *Reading is individual and silent,* at the student's own pace, and, outside class, done when and where the student chooses.

8. *Reading speed is usually faster rather than slower* as students read books and other material they find easily understandable.

9. *Teachers orient students to the goals of the program, explain* the methodology, *keep track* of what each student reads, and *guide* students in getting the most out of the program.

10. *The teacher is a role model of a reader for students*—an active member of the classroom reading community, demonstrating what it means to be a reader and the rewards of being a reader.

Day and Bamford, pp. 7–8

It is my belief that good readers do more extensive reading than intensive reading. But, what makes the reader a good reader is that he/she has developed the strategies and skills through intensive reading that are then transferred to extensive reading contexts. These ideas should give us, as reading teachers, cause to pause and consider the ratio of intensive and extensive reading activities we ask our students to engage in and see if we are providing opportunities for both types of reading.

---

5 *Consider the ideas presented above on intensive and extensive reading. Which of these two ways of approaching the teaching of reading do you see yourself gravitating toward? Can you identify why you feel you gravitate to one or the other? Record your ideas in your Reflective Reading Journal.*

---

6 *Consider how you could balance both intensive and extensive reading in your teaching. In what ways could you use both to strengthen reading comprehension skills of the students you are working with? Record your thoughts in your Reflective Reading Journal.*

The majority of the techniques we have discussed so far in this chapter have been tied to intensive reading. We have taken a short reading passage and have introduced readers to development of comprehension skills and strategies. A final area of research that can be addressed within the context of reading for comprehension is the research that is being conducted in the area of Content-Based Language Instruction (CBI). CBI moves readers away from intensive reading to more extensive reading. CBI is based on the assumption that learning a second language is not an end in and of itself. Language is learned in order to learn other things, such as social studies, biology, computer science, and math.

Content-based instruction

Recall what Paul Hardin said about this in the chapter on cultivating vocabulary. He involves the students in reading content area texts. He wants the readers to integrate their knowledge of content with the development of vocabulary skills and additional reading strategies. He also points out how the use of the content area reading material seems to increase students' motivation and create a real purpose for improving their reading skills and strategies. When readers make this connection, more learning occurs.

I have been influenced by the work of David and Yvonne Freeman (1992), Snow (1994), Chamot and O'Malley (1994), Peregoy and Boyle (1997) and Stoller and Grabe (1997). Freeman and Freeman (1992) highlight the similarities between CBI and whole language instruction:

> ESL learners need more than language drills or exercises designated to develop communicative competence. They do not have years to practice English before they acquire academic knowledge. They need to be offered an education that allows them to learn English through meaningful content so they can achieve academic and social success, and that is the goal of whole language teachers for the second language students. (p. 104)

Content-based instruction is a very appropriate instructional strategy at the secondary level. ESL teachers can provide a meaningful context for teaching reading comprehension strategies to students from the foundation of the content areas they are studying in other high school classes.

Freeman and Freeman (1992) continue to influence my thinking of the value of teaching reading comprehension skills through CBI when they point out that

> [t]he popular view that whole language means literacy instruction for elementary students is too narrow. Whole language extends to math, science, social studies, and all the content areas and to secondary as well as elementary education. Whole language means instruction that centers on students' needs and interests. Teachers applying whole language with second language students teach language through content because they recognize the importance of their students' developing not only language but also academic competence. Whole language without content instruction is not whole language. (p. 107)

7 *What do you know about whole language instruction? Does it fit into your philosophy of teaching ESL/EFL reading? Why or why not? Discuss your response with a colleague.*

Working collaboratively with content teachers

One important aspect for the ESL teacher to understand is that he or she is not replacing the content teacher but organizing language instruction around the topics from content area classes. Language teachers can select a content area topic and then develop language instructional strategies by identifying what elements of language naturally emerge from the topic.

Using CBI also provides a natural collaboration between content area teachers and the ESL teacher in a secondary or university school setting. Snow (1994) has directed the Learning English-for-Academic-Purposes (LEAP) project at California State University in Los Angeles. Many of the things that she and her colleagues have learned through their work can benefit both secondary and university level ESL/EFL teachers who are interested in working with content based teachers in their schools. Snow explains four major components of the LEAP project:

> 1) Study group courses, team-taught by peer study group leaders and language specialists, which are paired with selected general education courses; 2) Faculty development training to assist instructors to incorporate language sensitivity and academic literacy skill instruction into their general education courses; 3) Curriculum modification to institutionalize language-sensitive instruction into the targeted general education courses; and 4) Project continuity and dissemination to train future faculty and study group leaders and share project results both at CSLA (California State - Los Angeles) and with other colleges and universities around the country. (p. 4)

In my opinion, it is the third component of the LEAP model that is of value to any ESL/EFL reading teacher interested in CBI. We can analyze the language sensitive elements of a reading passage and organize our CBI around them.

---

8 *Select a content topic from which you could select a reading passage. Review the text and determine what language-sensitive elements you would want to highlight in your reading class to teach reading comprehension. Record your ideas in your Reflective Reading Journal.*

Investigations

Frameworks

Cognitive Academic Language Learning

Chamot and O'Malley (1994) have made a significant contribution to CBI with their Cognitive Academic Language Learning Approach (CALLA). Their handbook provides specific content applications for second language learners in science, mathematics, social studies, and language arts. Chamot and O'Malley outline three major components for CALLA: the selection of content topics, the development of academic language skills and the explicit instruction of learning strategies for both language learning and content learning. The second component of the CALLA approach, the development of academic language skills, is one aspect of importance for our consideration in teaching reading comprehension skills and CBI. Chamot and O'Malley point out that

> [l]anguage is used as a functional tool for learning academic subject matter. Students learn not just the vocabulary and grammar of the content area but also learn important concepts and skills using academic language. Students learn the language unctions that are important for performing effectively in the content area, such as *analyzing, evaluating, justifying,* and *persuading.* Students develop academic language skills in English through cognitively demanding activities in which comprehension is assessed by contextual supports and in which scaffolded instruction guides the acquisition of content. (p. 11)

9 *What overlap do you see in Snow's approach in the LEAP project and Chamot and O'Malley's CALLA approach? Is this information beneficial to you as a second language reading teacher? Why or why not? Discuss your ideas with a colleague.*

Creating optimal content learning

Peregoy and Boyle (1997) discuss the valuable role that content learning plays in the integration of all language skills. CBI is a very appropriate model for consideration in secondary level ESL classes. Based on a CBI project conducted in an ESL class, Peregoy and Boyle identify six elements that create optimal content learning for English language learners:

1. *Meaning and Purpose:* The topic was meaningful to the students; they selected it and helped shape its development.

2. *Prior knowledge:* Learning was built on prior knowledge and direct experience such as field trips.

3. *Integration of Opportunities to Use Language and Literacy for Learning Purposes:* Oral and written language were used to acquire knowledge and present it to others.

4. *Scaffolding for Support:* Scaffolds were provided, including group work, process writing, and direct experiences for learning.

5. *Collaboration:* Students collaborated to build knowledge and organize it for summarizing in a book.

6. *Variety:* Variety was built in at every step, with oral language, reading, writing, field trips, class discussions, guest speakers, and other avenues of learning provided. (p. 283)

These elements highlight the integrated nature of learning and how fitting reading into an overall curriculum can facilitate both language learning and content learning. CBI lends itself to natural extensive reading opportunities.

10 *What is your reaction to the six elements presented above by Peregoy and Boyle? How does extensive reading fit into the CBI context? What could you use from these elements in determining if you can implement CBI? Record your ideas in your Reflective Reading Journal.*

The Six T's

Stoller and Grabe (1997) provide what I consider a very effective approach for CBI entitled the Six T's approach. The six T's include

- Themes: organization for units in a curriculum

- Texts: material to be used for language instruction

- Topics: sub-units of content which allow the theme to be exploited for language teaching

- Threads: connection between various themes used in a curriculum

- Tasks: instructional activities to teach language and content

- Transitions: mechanism for planning how to move from one topic to another or from one theme to another in the curriculum

Each of these elements of the approach allows for the natural development of a CBI curriculum to meet the reading comprehension needs of second language learners. If your language program were to use Stoller and Grabe's Six T's approach, the CBI curriculum would integrate the teaching of reading comprehension based on the themes, topics, and texts you select. This provides what I consider an ideal curriculum for teaching of reading comprehension skills.

---

11 *How could you use Stoller and Grabe's Six T's approach to teach reading comprehension skills? What advantages do you see of this approach over other possible approaches to CBI? Discuss your ideas with a colleague.*

Based on the research literature, I have identified several classroom applications for teaching reading comprehension skills. I am not suggesting that these are the techniques that all reading teachers implement, but I do think that there is value in considering if any of these techniques would work for you as you seek to teach reading comprehension skills.

Possible classroom activities to teach for comprehension

One technique I have used is to get readers to monitor their comprehension while reading by periodically stopping and asking themselves: Why am I reading this material? What do I hope to learn? Do I understand what I am reading? Specifically, what am I doing right now to comprehend what I'm reading? If I'm not understanding what I'm reading, what else could I do to comprehend?

Monitor comprehension

Second, I get readers to formulate questions of their own. This classroom activity can be implemented in several ways. Readers can ask questions about material they do not understand and about which they would like to seek clarification from the teacher and/or classmates. This allows each reader to identify what is not understood and thus increases comprehension by obtaining an answer. Often the first step in teaching for comprehension is to ask readers to identify what is not comprehended.

Formulate questions

A third classroom activity I use to teach for comprehension is to have the reader summarize a reading passage or partial passage. The value of this teaching tool is that, in providing the summary, the reader needs to be able to distinguish between different levels of importance in the text: main ideas, supporting ideas, and details. An effective summary would demonstrate that a reader sees the difference among these different levels and can place emphasis at the proper level.

Summarize reading

Next, I review with the students common transition words they will encounter while reading. I share with them a list of commonly used transition words such as the following from the *Reference Guide to English: A Handbook of English as a Second Language* (Maclin, A. [1996]. Washington, D.C.: United States Information Agency).

Identify transition words

To add information and reasons	To show cause and effect	To explain, give reasons
also	accordingly	actually
besides	as a consequence	admittedly
equally	as a result	certainly
further	consequently	for example
furthermore	then	in fact
in addition	therefore	indeed
moreover	thus	really
too		of course
		that is

To compare	To contrast	To summarize
by comparison	however	in all
likewise	instead	in a word
similarly	in spite of that	in brief
	anyhow	briefly
	nevertheless	in short
	on the contrary	in summary
	on the other hand	
	otherwise	
	still	

To show order

First, second, . . .
Finally
last

To show chronological order

subsequently	then	first
later	now	formerly
next	nowadays	earlier
after that	concurrently	previously
afterwards	simultaneously	before that

Justify comprehension

Another application for the classroom is one that I have found especially helpful. I ask students to read a passage; then I ask comprehension questions or use the questions that often accompany passages in commercial texts. I then ask the class to justify their answers to the comprehension questions. In the process of justifying why they have answered the way they did, I get them to articulate how they arrived at the answer. One very interesting thing that has occurred in the process of doing this activity is that sometimes students have the wrong answer to begin with, and in the process of explaining to me and the class how they arrived at their answer the students discover on their own that what they thought was the correct answer is not correct at all. I do not have to point out that they have the wrong answer; they discover it for themselves. This justification exercise works well in teaching comprehension skills.

A final classroom application to consider is the relationship between the ideas we have discussed in this section on teaching comprehension skills with those in the previous sections of this text. Recall the image of a tapestry that we discussed in the Introduction to the Teaching Strategies section at the beginning of the book. Consider the interconnectedness of activating background knowledge, cultivating vocabulary skills, and teaching for comprehension. I have asked readers to use the title of a reading passage and make predictions about what they think they will be reading. Then we generate a list of potential vocabulary we think we will encounter. I will often explicitly introduce some specific vocabulary if the students do not suggest it themselves. We then discuss how the reading passage will be organized and what transition words we think we will see. Next, we will skim the passage by reading the first paragraph, the first sentence in the middle paragraphs and the entire last paragraph. We pause to ask questions and to verify if the hypothesis we made before skimming needs to be adjusted. Then I ask the class to read the passage for comprehension. Having gone through the sequence of integrated activities of activation of background knowledge, vocabulary, text organization, transition words, and skimming I believe that I am getting readers to identify the strategies they can use to monitor their comprehension while they are reading.

The value of teaching for comprehension activities in a reading classroom cannot be underestimated. Multiple choice tests can be developed to test comprehension, but the classroom teacher may want to explore ways to focus on teaching activities which teach rather than test comprehension.

Identify relationship among ideas

---

12 *Meet with a second language reader. From a reading text the student is currently using, choose a passage the student has not yet read. Ask the student to formulate three questions based on the title of the reading. Then read the passage together. Are the three questions the student generated answered in the text? Prepare three additional questions after reading the material.*

---

13 *Meet with a second language reader. From a reading text the student is currently using, choose a passage the student has not yet read. Ask the student to read a passage. Ask the student to then summarize the material. Watch carefully for the information the student reports. Does he/she report the main idea? What is the ratio of supporting ideas and details reported? Record your reactions to this experience in your Reflective Reading Journal.*

---

14 *Select a reading passage that contains transition words. Meet with a second language reader. Ask if he/she knows the purpose of transition words. If the reader does not know, discuss the function of transition words and provide some examples from the list on page 47. Ask the student to read the passage you have selected which contains transition words. Then discuss the reader's com-*

prehension using the transition words as a way to get the reader to recall the ideas in the passage. What do you learn from this investigation? Record your ideas in your Reflective Reading Journal.

CONCLUDING THOUGHTS

Think back to the art of bonsai and my experience of beginning this new hobby. In the early phases of the hobby I failed. I attribute this to two things. First, I think I tried to hurry the maturing process for the little tree too quickly. Second, I had to turn the nurturing over to someone else in the early stages of the process.

I have learned two things from this experience that have proven helpful in the development of my philosophy of teaching reading. First, I cannot rush the process of reading comprehension too quickly. Second language learners need time to learn how to integrate their own knowledge with the topic of the reading passage. They need time to apply new strategies that they are learning. Rushing them to be mature readers may have a negative impact. Second, I want to make sure I am prepared to nurture students through the process. The nurturing of reading comprehension skills requires one to be consistent over time and allow the learners the proper environment in which grow.

Suggested Readings

Bill Grabe (1997) provides essential information in an article entitled "Discourse Analysis and Reading Instruction" published in a volume by the United States Information Agency. The contribution of this article deals with how text organization influences comprehension instruction. We can accomplish the teaching for comprehension by instructing learners how knowing about the text organization can improve their overall reading comprehension.

Harrison's "The Reading Process and Learning to Read" in *The Reading for Real Handbook* (1992) provides valuable insights into how interactive reading models can be modified based on research. In order for teachers to significantly contribute to teaching comprehension skills, it is my belief that an understanding of the reading process will facilitate our ability to teach. This article may be of interest.

For an insightful treatment on how to integrate content based instruction into your teaching you might find a chapter by Fredrika Stoller and Bill Grabe (1997) of interest. They propose what they call the six T's approach to content based instruction. This chapter in a wonderful volume edited by Marguerite Ann Snow and Donna M. Brinton entitled *The Content-based Classroom: Perspectives on Integrating Language and Content* may have additional material that you would find helpful.

Day and Bamford have an entire text on the topic of extensive reading, *Extensive Reading in the Second Language Classroom* (1998). Of particular value in the book is a section on the practice of extensive reading. Check out this valuable resource.

A final very interesting piece which will provide the L1 perspective comes from J. F. Baumann (1984) in an article published in *Reading Research Quarterly* that examines the issue of direct instruction for teaching main idea comprehension.

As language teachers it is my belief that we need to move away from the testing of comprehension and teach the readers we work with how to develop strong reading comprehension skills. These articles may provide you with some interesting food for thought.

5

STRATEGY FOUR

INCREASE READING RATE

1 *Give your definition of reading rate. Do you believe that reading rate is an important skill for second language readers? Why or why not? Record your definition and reasoning in your Reflective Reading Journal.*

Investigations

2 *Interview an ESL/EFL teacher and ask her or him to define reading rate. Does she or he believe that reading rate is an important skill for second language readers? Why or why not? Record what you have learned from this interview in your Reflective Reading Journal.*

Let me share how I "discovered" the principle of automaticity. As a graduate student at the University of Texas at Austin, I often drove my car to school. One beautiful fall afternoon I left campus to drive home. It was late in the afternoon, about 6:00 p.m. The sky was a crystal clear blue. I listened to the radio and enjoyed the drive home. My mind wandered as I thought about the beauties of the day and about the tasks I had to complete.

Teachers' Voices

As I drove into the driveway of my home and shut the car off I sat in amazement. I didn't remember crossing the bridge. I didn't remember taking the exit from the freeway. I didn't remember turning on my blinkers, although I am confident that I did because it was my habit to do so. At first I was a bit scared. What if every other driver on the road that afternoon had the same experience I had? Isn't this a bit dangerous?

I didn't give the matter additional thought as I entered my home and put the day of university studies behind me.

The next morning I left early to teach my 8:00 a.m. ESL writing course. As I left the house it was raining. I jumped into the car and got it started. I turned on the windshield wipers and nothing happened! What! No wipers! How am I going to drive to campus without wipers?

I backed out of the driveway. Before I even made it to the first corner I had to shut off the radio. (It was still on from the pleasant drive home the previous afternoon.) As I turned each corner I was very much aware of turning on my blinkers. My speed was very slow as other cars whizzed by me in the rain. I realized that if I sat very low in the seat I had a bit of visibility directly under the edge of the windshield wiper. I also rolled down the window in order to see the white lines of my lane on the highway pavement.

There I sat, driving very slowly on the interstate, getting drenched from the rain, sitting low in my seat trying to navigate my way to campus. I remember passing several dead armadillos. I remember being very much aware of the weight of my foot on the accelerator. When I arrived at the campus parking lot, I was exhausted!

After I taught my class I began to reflect on these two driving experiences and then the connection of automaticity became very clear to me.

When conditions are proper, with no interference, we sail along with perfect comfort, not thinking about what we are doing. Automaticity takes control of the "regular" actions we complete. When conditions become less than favorable, we suddenly become very aware of what we are doing. I wouldn't have been able to tell you what I did the afternoon I drove home under perfect conditions. But if you were to ask me what I did the morning of the rain storm, driving with no windshield wipers, I would have been able to tell you everything I did and give great detail about every inch of highway between my home and the university.

Frameworks

Automaticity in reading

Understanding the concept of automaticity is of great value to a second language reading teacher. Often our students are trying to focus on too many reading tasks at the same time and do not comprehend what they are reading. In addition, their reading rate is very slow, which also results in not understanding what they have read. Increasing students' reading rates makes them able to devote greater cognitive capacity to comprehension skills.

As we investigate the role of reading rate in second language instruction, I am not suggesting that we get readers to *speed read* thousands of words per minute. I am suggesting that we get our readers to read fluently and automatically. This has been an important issue for me as a reading teacher since I continually notice that students in my ESL classes lack automaticity and fluency in their reading rates.

As a classroom reading teacher I examined materials to see how to develop the reading rate of the learners in my classes. I was greatly disappointed to see that the most common instruction given to learners was, "*read the following as quickly as possible.*" My personal philosophy of learning and teaching did not accept that as the way to go about developing reading fluency in second language readers.

We'll examine my beliefs and the beliefs of two other teachers. I'll share with you four specific reading rate development activities I've used to increase automaticity of text recognition to help second language readers move beyond word level reading to fluent processing of large quantities of text.

Teachers' Voices

Teaching reading is not new for Dawn Turton, but the concept of increasing students' reading rates is. She continues to gain insights into her own teaching as she reflects on helping her students increase their reading rates.

Before teaching here in the U.S. I had not really given much thought to the idea of reading rate. This is not something that was emphasized in my education in Britain. Is speed reading something taught in U.S. schools? This is a very new concept to me.

I observed a colleague teaching an intermediate reading class. He talked about increasing reading rate with his class. I have also heard other teachers talking about getting their students to increase their reading speed. I've heard them discuss it so I knew that there was concern about increasing rate.

This is now the second quarter of teaching reading. I see that using rate-building activities helps increase student motivation. For two of my students in particular, they can see that their reading speed is double what it was at the beginning of the quarter. They are so pleased when they turn in their timed reading pages. They point it out to me. Students will say to me, "Look what I read in three minutes!" All these issues tie into motivation.

Dawn has pointed out in her comment here the important nature of the interconnectedness of these issues. We will discuss the role of motivation later in the book (see Chapter 8: Build Motivation). It is difficult to discuss reading rate in isolation from the other issues discussed in this book. Dawn continues:

I discussed the importance of reading rates with several of my students from the part-time level reading class. All the students were aware of their reading rates, as this is an area which is focused on in our classes. However, not all students believed that their reading rate was important. They thought that the reading rate was dependent on the material they were reading, and that when reading for academic purposes, it is important to read slowly and to read every word. I've noticed that some of the students move a pencil along every word when they read, and I have been trying to make the students aware that this slows down their reading rate. However, my efforts have met with a mixed response. The students have a fear of losing comprehension if they speed up their reading rates. To help them increase their reading rate and read for comprehension, I use the timed readers and also some timed reading exercises from several reading books. I'm also focusing on scanning and skimming exercises to get them to read in different ways and to try and increase their reading rate.

Notice how Dawn has addressed the topic of reading rate with her students. As part of any discussion in a reading class it is important to get the students' perspective. Perhaps they have opinions about the "theory" we are "pushing" in our reading class.

Dawn continues by discussing a few of the things that she has used in class to help students understand the importance of increasing their reading rates:

One way I tried to make the students aware of the benefits of an increased reading rate was to use a diagram which illustrates how many books a fast reader can get through. The problem is that the students are currently taking only one academic class and consequently they can spend a long time on the required readings.

However, they need to increase their reading rate in preparation for an increased academic load.

When they move into content area reading tasks, ESL/EFL students benefit from a fluent reading rate because they will have increased reading demands. A new immigrant in a 9th grade social studies class may experience for the first time an increase in the amount of material she must read and understand in English. An international student enrolled in an intensive reading program preparing to enter the university will need to develop fluent, automatic reading in order to cover the material assigned by professors. An EFL learner studying at home in Egypt will want to develop a fluent reading rate in order to read more scientific material in his field of study. Increasing reading rate will allow students to move through the heavy reading assignments that accompany university study.

Increased reading fluency can also improve performance on standardized tests. ESL/EFL learners are faced with many formal testing situations where reading rate plays a critical role in being able to complete the task in the time allotted. Students also see the benefits of increasing reading rate for this purpose. Let's look at how this helped Dawn.

> Students report that their TOEFL scores are low. So I ask why they think their TOEFL reading scores are low. They respond that they can't get through all of the passages. I ask why they think they can't get through all of the passages. They indicate that there are too many questions. I tell them that the number of questions on the TOEFL is not going to change. So, what has to change? I ask them. Then they say, oh, maybe if we read a bit faster.

Teachers'
Voices

Let's now listen to another teacher's voice. Carolyn O'Keeffe works with ESL teachers and Instructional Assistants in Northshore School District, Bothell, Washington as the District Pre-K–12 ESL Coordinator. At the University of Washington in ESL education courses, she also works with certification and pre-service teachers.

> In all of my work with both groups, reading rate has been a strong focus of coursework and workshops. Increasing student reading rate is essential if students are going to succeed in their academic work as well as becoming more fluent, fluid readers of English. I am seeing more students enrolling in our schools with not only limited English language ability, but also limited reading and writing ability or fluency in their own first languages. We are enrolling students in the secondary schools who have very little schooling experience in their own countries. Reading is one of the most important language skills for ensuring student success at all educational levels. Knowing how to read more efficiently and adjusting reading speed to reading task are critical to this success. Because of the factors mentioned above, starting with timed readings of fixed rate or fixed amount of reading is too advanced for many of our students. At both the elementary and secondary levels, I help teachers to begin with increasing reading rate, but at the tiniest step: rapid number recog-

nition. We build automaticity at this beginning level where students feel some comfort. Here is a sample:

8			9	7	8	6	3
4			3	4	5	7	9
11			12	21	10	11	17

Students see a set of ten items, like the three above. Their task is to find the number within the group on the right that matches the number to the left. The teacher times this activity. I suggest doing several sets of ten, increasing the speed as students become more automatic in recognizing the numbers. From here, we move to rapid letter recognition. The task is the same: several sets of ten completed quickly. After letter recognition, teachers move students to consonant blends, to vowels, and to words. Both elementary and secondary beginning readers find these activities fun. There is a sense of fun and a game-like quality to completing these tasks. Teachers often use them as warm up activities at the beginning of a lesson or quick reviews at the end. These tasks last no longer than ten minutes.

From rapid word recognition, teachers move students into rapid phrase recognition activities. In this type of activity, students are looking for the "key phrase" in a group of phrases. For example, they read, "key phrase: buy lunch." They are then told to circle this key phrase every time they read it in the activity, such as the one below:

buy lunch	take a lunch	make lunch	bring lunch
buy milk	buy lunch	buy lunches	bake lunch
bring lunch	take lunch	find lunch	buy lunch

The teacher is timing them. Each consecutive rapid phrase activity can increase in speed as students become more successful and adept at reading in chunks of language. This is their first practice of reading in chunks for reading comprehension and reading rate improvement.

After students have had practice in reading and finding key phrases, we move to practicing "chunking" with a short one-hundred-word passage. I have teachers practice underlining chunks of language within the passage in an effort to find the natural flow and connection of words and thoughts of the writer. We discuss the differences we may have among our "chunked out" passage. This leads to a rich discussion of what a natural or reasonable chunk of language is and how it may differ depending on level of reading and language fluency. The teachers go back and try this same activity with their students. Second language learners often read word for word. This activity helps them to practice the chunking process that fluent readers do automatically. It offers teachers and students the opportunity to discuss the importance of chunking when reading and how it helps in increasing reading speed and comprehension of what is being read. ESL students have shared how this activity helped them to make sense out of all the words on the page. At the elementary level, many members of my ESL staff are using CD-ROM programs from Broderbund. Students love these interactive stories and so do the teachers. What students see on the screen matches the chunking practice that they have completed in class. As the students watch the actions and hear the character or narrator talk, the words of the story for that page are highlighted in chunks or phrases. They practice reading in chunks! They have visual and aural modeling of this skill.

Once students have practiced and can understand how reading in chunks facilitates better comprehension and fluency, we can move on to timed readings. I suggest that teachers utilize readings from the students' content area classes. Teachers try both fixed rate and variable rate approaches. We also try a different approach to the repeated reading activity. First, teachers have students skim the passage for the "gist" of the reading. Then, teachers have the students scan it for 3 or 4 specific details. The last step is to have students read it at a timed reading rate. Students discuss how much faster they were able to read and comprehend the passage after skimming and scanning it first.

Another activity we practice that is related to increasing reading rates is helping students to move away from using their finger, pencil, or pen as a reading guide. Many students tell their teachers how lost they would be without using their pen or pencil while reading. There is a sea of words and their pencil acts as a beacon. What I have students practice is moving their pencil to the end of the line of reading. When they come to the end, they move their pencil down to the end of the next line and so on. Once they reach this comfort level, teachers have students make their own book-marks and these are then laminated. With their new bookmarks, students practice placing the bookmark at the line they are reading and moving the marker down one line once they come to the end of each line. Students practice reading exposing one line of text at a time. The next step is to move the bookmark down to the end of the paragraph. Now, one whole paragraph or small section of text is in the student's reading sight. They still have comfort in that they are not lost in a sea of print. They are increasing their reading rate as they become more confident in this technique. Students have shared with their ESL teachers how this technique helps them to focus more on the content shown. They rarely revert to using the pencil, pen, or finger to keep their place. Of course, the next step is to move the bookmark down to the bottom of the page so that all the text is exposed.

I have had EFL teachers from Japan, Korea, and China come up to me and tell me how much better they can read in English after practicing all of these activities. Reading their graduate level course materials became easier for them as they highlighted chunks of language and used a bookmark as a guide for focusing on specific amounts of text.

I have been influenced in my thinking of reading rate by some of the research that has been done. Surprisingly, a review of the research in the area of second language reading rate results in very few studies. The few studies that exist do provide us with very interesting information. Data from Segalowitz, Poulsen, and Komoda (1991) indicate that second language reading rates of highly bilingual readers are "30% or more slower than L1 reading rates" (p. 15). These data are also supported by Weber (1991), who points out that highly skilled bilinguals typically have a slower reading rate in their second language. Average ESL readers are well below average native speakers of English in reading ability. Slow reading speed constitutes a serious handicap for L2 readers when they commence studying in content areas in English. Data from Jensen (1986) indicates that even after studying reading, many advanced ESL students may read only 100 words per minute or less. To many second language readers, reading is a suffocatingly slow process. Explicit instruction in rapid reading is an area which is often neglected in the classroom. The discussion and activities to increase reading rate suggested here are not designed to have second language readers read thousands of words per minute, but to increase their reading rate to a satisfactory level to be successful in academic reading tasks.

Reading rate
research studies

Cushing Weigle and Jensen (1996) reported on a reading rate development study conducted at UCLA. Reading rate instruction was integrated into the academic multiskills course for international students at UCLA. These advanced readers began the quarter at an average rate of 184 words per minute (wpm). After nine weeks of instruction in regular timed and paced readings the students' reading rate increased more than 100 wpm with some of the readers having improved as many as 400 wpm. The authors report that the increase in rate was statistically significant at p<.05 based on a matched t-test. This is one of the few empirical studies investigating the impact of reading rate instruction in second language reading classes.

Nuttall (1996) describes the frustration that may be part of slower reading in her description of the "vicious cycle of the weak reader" (p. 127). Readers who do not understand often slow down their reading rate and then do not enjoy reading because it takes so much time. Therefore, they do not read much. These readers continue in the vicious cycle. By increasing reading rate, Nuttall suggests that the reader can get into the "virtuous cycle of the good reader" (ibid.). By reading faster, the reader is encouraged to read more and, with more reading, comprehension improves.

---

3 *What do you believe an "adequate" reading rate is? Interview an ESL/EFL reading teacher and ask her what the reading rates are of her students.*

Grabe (1991) states that "fluent reading is rapid; the reader needs to maintain the flow of information at a sufficient rate to make connections and inferences vital to comprehension" (p. 378). Conflicting data exist regarding the optimal or sufficient reading rate. Some authorities suggest that 180 words per minute "may be a threshold between immature and mature reading, that a speed

Optimal
reading rate

below this is too slow for efficient comprehension or for the enjoyment of text" (Higgins and Wallace, 1989, p. 392). Dubin and Bycina (1991) state that "a rate of 200 words per minute would appear to be the absolute minimum in order to read with full comprehension" (p. 198). Jensen (1986) recommends that second language readers seek to "approximate native speaker reading rates and comprehension levels in order to keep up with classmates" (p. 106). She suggests that 300 words per minute is the optimal rate. This rate is supported by Nuttall, (1982) who states that "for an L1 speaker of English of about average education and intelligence . . . the reading rate is about 300 w.p.m. The range among L1 speakers is very great; rates of up to 800 w.p.m. and down to 140 w.p.m. are not uncommon" (p. 36).

Carver (1990, p. 14) proposed five reading processes, and each has a typical rate. These five processes and typical rates include:

Reading process	Processing components	Target WPM
Scanning	Lexical accessing	600
Skimming	Semantic encoding	450
Rauding	Sentence integrating	300
Learning	Idea remembering	200
Memorizing	Fact rehearsing	138

"Rauding" is a term that Carver coined. It is defined as "comprehension of all or almost all of the consecutively encountered thoughts during reading or auding; comprehending about 75% or more of the complete thoughts encountered during the operation of the rauding process" (Carver, 1990, p. 467). Carver states that this is "representative of what is often called natural, normal, typical, or ordinary reading" (p. 16). This suggests then that 300 wpm is the rate at which efficient reading takes place. If we are reading faster or slower than 300 wpm we are not *reading*; we would be scanning, skimming, learning, or memorizing the material.

I am not sure that Carver would agree with this, but this suggests to me that importance of adjusting the reading rate according to the task at hand. Carolyn mentioned in the Teachers' Voices section on page 55 the importance for her of teaching students how to adjust their reading speed to the reading task. Carver does suggest that if you are reading fewer than 300 words per minute you are not really *reading* but learning or memorizing. This seems to suggest that rate adjustment fits the purpose for engaging in the material you are covering: skimming, scanning, reading/listening, learning, or memorizing.

Based on the review of literature on the issue of adequate reading rates, I have set class goals at 200 words per minute. This has proven to be a reasonable goal to work toward without being too overwhelming to students.

4 *What is your reaction to Carver's research on reading rate? Do you agree with his statements? Why or why not? Record your thoughts in your Reflective Reading Journal.*

Possible classroom activities to increase reading rate

During the 1960s and 1970s, there were four significant recommendations regarding pedagogical techniques for rapid reading. Harris (1966) provided exercises in word recognition, vocabulary building, as well as selections used for timed reading in his text *Reading Improvement Exercises for Students of English as a Second Language*. He also provided exercises in skimming and scanning. Students were given instructions to read the passage as quickly as possible. Plaister (1968) on the other hand, suggested the use of a metronome in improving reading speed. The metronome was used as a pacer with a 3x5 index card to read through teacher prepared materials. The goal was to read a line of text in one fixation of the eye, then moving to the next line with the beat of the metronome. In contrast, Seliger (1972) proposed a method of previewing, scanning, directed reading, and using the finger as a pacer to reduce eye regressions. Finally, Riley (1975) proposed a method she referred to as "phrase reading." This method, similar to the one proposed by Plaister, advocated teaching students to increase their eye span by reading in units. Instructions were given to focus on an imaginary vertical line down the center of the page and through use of the eye span to read the material. Riley also advocated the use of reading machines that assist in pacing the reader.

It is these kinds of activities in the reading class that Carolyn referred to earlier in this chapter on pages 55–56. These kinds of rate-building exercises have been very effective for her in her teaching. And her students seem to have benefited a great deal from them.

These four methods rely upon the use of mechanical devices, specially prepared materials by the teacher, or simple instructions to "read as quickly as possible." Psycholinguistic research indicates that increasing eye span is not really the problem (Carpenter & Just, 1986; Rayner & Pollatsek, 1989). Instead further effort could be devoted to improving the efficiency of word recognition during the eye fixations. Grabe (1991) reviews studies that explain the eye movement data and indicates that "80% of content words and 40% of function words are directly focused on in reading" (p. 385). Although these activities do help in developing reading skills, students do not learn to increase their reading rates significantly through these methods.

The following four reading rate activities can be used in the second language reading class to increase student reading rate. These activities do not require that the teacher prepare any special materials for the students to practice. No special equipment is required. The texts that are used as part of the reading class can be used for these rate-building exercises or students may bring their own reading materials to class to practice rate building.

BLACKBURN COLLEGE LIBRARY

Rate Buildup Reading. Students are given sixty seconds to read as much material as they can. They then begin reading again from the beginning of the text and are given an additional sixty seconds. They are to read more material during the second sixty second period than in the first. The drill is repeated a third and a fourth time. The purpose of this activity is to reread "old" material quickly, gliding into the new. As the eyes move quickly over the "old" material the students actually learn how to get their eyes moving at a faster reading rate. The exercise involves more than simply moving the eyes quickly, the material should be processed and comprehended. As students participate in this rate building activity, they learn to increase reading rate.

Repeated Reading. Students read a short passage over and over again until they achieve criterion levels of reading rate and comprehension. For example, they may try to read a short 100-word paragraph four times in two minutes. The criterion levels may vary from class to class, but reasonable goals to work towards are criterion levels of 200 words per minute at 70% comprehension. Results of studies with native speakers of English indicate that

> as the student continued to use this technique, the initial speed of reading each new selection was faster than initial speed on the previous selection. Also, the number of rereadings required to reach the criterion reading speed decreased as the student continued the technique. . . . [This seems to indicate] a transfer of training and a general improvement in reading fluency. (Samuels, 1979, p. 404)

Teachers'
Voices

Dawn tried the Reading Rate Buildup and the Repeated Reading activities in her class. Look at what she says:

> I use Rate Buildup Reading and Repeated Reading. I found that the students really enjoyed it. I used it when we first started talking about reading rate.

> Students would get to the second paragraph of a reading and say that they couldn't remember the first paragraph because they were reading so slowly. I use Rate Buildup reading for that reason to show them that if they read something through several times quickly then it will affect their comprehension. At first they didn't believe it.

> When I told them that they were going to be reading the same things several times they were sceptical. Their perception is that it will take them three times as long to read something three times. I told them it would increase their speed and they didn't believe me. I told them it would also increase their comprehension and they didn't believe that either.

> I tried a little experiment. I had one group read the passage one time in 5 minutes and answer comprehension questions. Another group read the same material three times in 5 minutes. The group that read three times had higher comprehension scores.

Class-Paced Reading. This activity requires a discussion regarding a class goal for minimal reading rate. Once that goal is established, the average number of words per page of the material being read is calculated. It is then determined how much material needs to be read in one minute in order to meet the class goal. For example, if the class goal is to read 250 words per minute and the material being read has an average of 125 words per page, the class would be expected to read one page every thirty seconds. As each thirty seconds elapses, the teacher indicates to the class to move to the next page. Students are encouraged to keep up with the established class goal. Of course, those who read faster than 250 wpm are not expected to slow down their reading rate. As long as they are ahead of the designated page they continue reading.

Self-Paced Reading. The procedures for this activity are very similar to the class-paced reading activity outlined above. During this reading rate activity the students determine their own goal for reading rate. They then determine how much material needs to be read in a sixty second period to meet their objective rate. For example, suppose a student's objective rate is 180 words per minute and that the material being read has an average number of 10 words per line. The student would need to read 18 lines of text in one minute to meet the goal. The activity proceeds nicely by having each student mark off several chunks of lines and silently read for a period of 5–7 minutes with the instructor calling out minute times. Students can then determine if they are keeping up with their individual reading rate goal.

Additional Activities. In addition to these four specific classroom reading rate activities, students can be given a variety of reading passages and multiple choice comprehension questions like those found in most rate-building texts. They can set individual goals for reading rate and reading comprehension. Students can be encouraged during these readings to work towards reading at least 200 words per minute with at least 70% comprehension.

Recall Carver's ideas that rate is closely tied to reading process. Reading material to comprehend, not to study or memorize, is at a rate of 300 wpm. When I ask second language readers in my classes to read at least 200 wpm, we use passages that are not intended to be studied or memorized. The reading level needs to be slightly below the level of language proficiency so that they can practice reading fluency, not learning of new material.

These rate-building activities seek to get the readers to a level of automatic processing of the text. Murtagh (1989) stresses that "good L2 reading is characterized by fast automatic word processing" (p. 102). LaBerge and Samuels (1974 [cited in Samuels, 1979]) state that the repeated reading techniques in particular "emerged largely from the teaching implications of the theory of automatic information processing in reading" (p. 406). Samuels continues by stating that

> according to automaticity theory, a fluent reader decodes text automatically—that is, without attention—thus leaving attention free to be used for comprehension. . . . One important function of repeated reading is that it provides the practice needed to become automatic. (p. 406)

Class-Paced Reading

Self-Paced Reading

For more on rate building see Fry, 1975; Harris, 1966; Spargo and Williston, 1980

Additional Activities

He emphasizes that "as less attention is required for decoding, more attention becomes available for comprehension. Thus rereading both builds fluency and enhances comprehension" (p. 405–406). This idea is also supported by Murtagh (1989). Segalowitz, Poulsen, and Komoda (1991) argue that "bilinguals who read more slowly in their L2 than in their L1 need to enhance the automaticity of word recognition processes in their L2 reading" (p. 7). The rapid reading activities outlined above can facilitate practice in building the automaticity skills needed in second language reading.

It is my belief that we need to get our students reading at least 200 words per minute. Some may argue that reading rates should vary according to the difficulty level of the material and the interest level of the students. I believe that is true only after we have reached a threshold level of reading rate, which I believe is around 200 wpm.

Fluency versus accuracy

Often, in our efforts to assist students in increasing their reading rate, teachers overemphasize accuracy at the expense of fluency, and when accuracy is overemphasized, reading fluency is impeded. The teacher must work towards a balance in reading rate improvement and reading comprehension. During some rate-building exercises the teacher may need to emphasize reading rate over reading comprehension.

Rate building with beginning level readers

The activities outlined above work very well with intermediate and advanced proficiency ESL/EFL learners. But what about the beginning level learner? At what point in the acquisition of second language reading skills is it appropriate to introduce reading rate?

The word recognition exercises proposed by Harris (1966) have been effective pedagogical tools for beginning level learners. Recall that my purpose for focusing on reading rate is not to get readers to read thousands of words per minute but to develop automaticity in word recognition so that their reading rate is such that they are focusing on meaningful connections between sentences and paragraphs. We can begin the focus on automaticity at the beginning levels at the letter and word units.

Following Harris' format a reading teacher could ask beginning level readers to complete an exercise like the following:

Look at the shape on the left. Circle the same shape on the right.

❐	|	▲	❐	◗	✳	○
▲	|	✛	☆	✳	▲	†
◯	|	✳	★	◯	✛	✘
✳	|	✢	♣	✳	✔	✕

The activity continues using letters:

| b | \| | b | p | d | \| | y |
| V | \| | W | M | Q | V | R |

then words:

| ball | \| | tall | call | wall | ball | fall |

building finally to phrases:

You're welcome | You're welcome   You are welcome   It is welcome

So reading rate and automaticity building can be taught with even beginning-level proficiency readers.

Look back at Paul Hardin's comments in the Teachers' Voices section on Cultivating Vocabulary (page 24). He uses activities like this to develop automaticity in word recognition. Carolyn also referred to activities like this with number recognition earlier in this chapter in her Teacher's Voice section (page 57).

Does any of this spill over to reading outside of the class? Listen to Dawn thinking:

> Although I know of no data gathered on the transfer of these classroom techniques to students' academic lives, I do believe from anecdoctal evidence that these techniques do have an impact on students' overall reading. Students report focusing on their reading rates long after they have completed my reading course.

The computer is a tool that reading teachers can use to provide another form of reading rate practice. *NewReader,* software developed by Hyperbole Software, includes two reading rate practice components: timed reading and paced reading. (Note that there are additional exercises that this software also provides.) The great advantage of *NewReader* is that teachers are able to scan in their own texts and allow students to practice using text material they are using in class. In the *Timed Reading* exercise the computer checks the reader's normal reading speed. In the *Paced Reading* exercise the computer shows the text at rates from 100 to 500 words-per-minute.

Computer software

Dawn comments on one reading rate improvement activity that seemed to be well received by her students:

> One activity that proved to be successful was getting the students to use the New Reader program on the computer. They seemed to enjoy having the opportunity to gradually increase their reading rate on the computer.

As reading teachers reflect upon the vital role of increasing students' reading rates, they will be in a better position to assist students improve their reading skills.

5 *Write Hyperbole Software for a demonstration copy of* NewReader. *At the time of publication of this book the address is 5 Sunnyside Drive, Athens, OH 45701-1919 USA. Telephone: (614) 594-4609. Try out the software. Have your class try the* Timed Reading *and* Paced Reading *exercises. What is the reaction to these reading rate practice opportunities? Record your reaction and your students' reactions in your Reflective Reading Journal.*

6 *Examine your own reading rate. Take a timed reading and learn what your average reading rate is. What was your reaction to your own reading rate? What is your reaction to this measurement?*

7 *Interview a second language reader about his/her reading rate. Is he/she aware of his/her reading rate? What has the learner done to improve his/her reading rate?*

8 *Interview an ESL/EFL reading teacher. What does she/he do to increase the reading rate of her/his learners? Do they believe that what they do is effective?*

9 *If you want to give all of the activities a fair trial, you might consider trying each of them with a group of ESL/EFL learners. You could devote a period of one month to using a variety of these activities and then assess their value in your class. Get the learners' reactions to the activities. Can you see an increase in reading rate after one month? If you decide any of the activities are inappropriate for your particular teaching situation, explain why. Record your reactions to these activities in your Reflective Reading Journal.*

CONCLUDING THOUGHTS

Automaticity plays a critical role in the development of strong reading skills. My belief is based on my own reading as well as watching students I have worked with over the years. When reading rate becomes more automatic, readers will be able to use their cognitive skills for comprehending what they are reading. They will be able to spend thinking time analyzing and synthesizing what they are reading and not moving through a passage one word at a time. The reader must approach the reading task with automaticized skills. She shouldn't have to be thinking about each of the steps involved in what she is doing. The good reader will approach the reading task much the way I approached driving home from the university that beautiful spring day. The joy of reading is being able to pick up a book and comprehend without having to struggle through the task.

Suggested Readings

Recall that what I have found frustrating as a reading teacher about the issue of reading rate is that there is not very much available to suggest to ESL/EFL teachers how to actually improve student reading rates. A 1979 article by S. J. Samuels in *The Reading Teacher* is one of the tools which I found which influenced my thinking about how I could adapt this technique of repeated readings for second language readers. You too may find this beneficial.

Ron Carver's *Reading Rate, a Review of Reasearch and Theory* (1990) presents a very interesting perspective on reading rate research with first language readers. I wish that more second language reading teachers were aware of his work and that we could begin a dialogue on how these issues relate to second language readers. See what you think after reading his work.

6

STRATEGY FIVE
VERIFY STRATEGIES

When I was in the sixth grade in elementary school, I remember the day that the teacher passed out announcements about the school orchestra. The music teacher from the Junior High School would be coming to our small elementary school once a week and working with children interested in being in an orchestra. What excitement! I walked home that day with two neighbor friends. They were each in the orchestra already. Kirsten played the viola and Peter played the cello. I was determined that I would join them in the orchestra.

At dinner that night I announced to my parents that I was joining the school orchestra. We had a piano and I was taking lessons, and I felt that I was ready now to expand my musical skills. My father responded that he did not want a squeaky violin in our home.

Up to that point I had not even given serious thought to what instrument I wanted to play. I just wanted to be in the orchestra. Before my father's response could dampen my eager enthusiasm I told him that I didn't intend to play the violin. I was going to play the string bass. The string bass? What a choice! I had made the announcement with such conviction and courage, and it wasn't a squeaky violin, so I think I caught my parents off guard. There were no objections. I joined the orchestra and began playing the string bass.

At the first meeting of the orchestra the teacher brought the large string bass for me to use. It was beautiful! I had never seen anything like it and neither had the other students at the elementary school. Because of its large size I knew I could not carry it back and forth often between my home and the school. I choose to practice before or after school in the building, rather than carry the instrument home.

At some point I wanted to spend some extra time practicing over the weekend so I carried the string bass home. I remember my father's reaction to my practicing. "What kind of music is that?" he asked. I wasn't sure how to answer his question. As I practiced I could "hear" the other instruments playing in my mind and I knew how my part fit into the overall pattern of the music. I knew that I was simply part of a greater whole. It was difficult for an 11-year-old to explain that to his father.

Then I started thinking. The string bass really isn't a very beautiful instrument when played by itself. There is real value in having a variety of instruments playing together to make real music. Knowing that what I was doing fit into the overall beauty of the music made me even more conscious of the beauty of the music. I remember thinking how poor the music sounded if the string bass was missing.

Understanding the interdependency of the string bass with the violins, violas, cellos, and other instruments in the orchestra was a very important learning experience for me.

Teachers' Voices

Dawn is in a situation where she is currently experimenting with some techniques for teaching language learning strategies. Look at what she has tried while teaching reading strategies.

> I have tried to teach strategies explicitly in my reading class. After administering a reading strategy questionnaire at the beginning of the quarter, I asked the students to talk about which strategies they use that are helpful in reading. They discuss this in small groups and we come up with a list of strategies which could be used to help students improve their reading. After a week I check to see if the students have tried to use any of the new strategies we had discussed and the students have admitted that in their out-of-class readings, they were reading in the same way as before. I then ask the students to read a passage and write down a step-by-step analysis of their reading process. The students then exchange this list with a partner, and the partner has to read the same passage in the same way as the first student. I used this technique both in in-class and in out-of-class assignments. Some of the class said they found this helpful as it enables them to use different strategies and they see how others approach reading and we are able to discuss why some strategies are more helpful than others.

> This week I'm looking at sentence study in my class. The students are using strategies to analyze long complicated sentences in order to extract the main idea. I have found the explicit instruction of strategies to be very beneficial in my reading class. However, I also think that it is an area that needs to be pursued over a greater period of time than a 10 week course. It would be interesting to observe these students next quarter when they are in full-time academic classes and see whether they are still using the strategies we have looked at.

Defining strategies

Strategies can be defined as "deliberate actions that learners select and control to achieve desired goals or objectives" (Winograd and Hare, 1988, p. 123). This definition underscores the active role that readers take in strategic reading. Students need to learn how to orchestrate the use of reading strategies to achieve the desired result. Garner, Macready, and Wagoner (1984) point out that "a strategy is a sequence of activities, not a single event and learners may have acquired some of the sequence, but not all" (p. 301).

Researchers have suggested that teaching readers how to use strategies is a prime consideration in the reading classroom. While teaching L2 readers how to use a given strategy, they must also be taught how to determine if they are successful in their use of that strategy. Garner (1982) emphasizes that low-proficiency readers need guided practice if strategy training is to be successful. Such training can emphasize the "when" and "why" of strategy use at least as much as the "what."

Recall our introduction to CALLA (Chamot & O'Malley, 1994) discussed earlier. Chamot and O'Malley include language strategy instruction as the "third and central component of CALLA" (p. 11). They stress the central role of explicit strategy instruction:

> We emphasize repeatedly that students who are mentally active and who analyze and reflect on their learning activities will learn, retain, and be able to use new information more effectively. Furthermore, students will be able to learn and apply strategies more effectively with new tasks if they verbalize and describe their efforts to apply strategies with learning activities. (p. 11)

We discussed earlier (Teaching Strategy 3: Teach for Comprehension) the value of verbalization of metacognitive awareness. Chamot and O'Malley stress this element in their approach also. We will discuss further in this chapter how we can use verbalization of strategies as an instructional tool.

For more on teaching strategies see Barnett, 1989; Carrell, Pharis, and Liberto, 1989; Chamot and O'Malley, 1994; Cohen, 1990; Kern, 1989; Oxford, 1989; Swaffar, Arens, and Byrnes, 1991

The role of teacher explanation is an integral part of success in learning how to verify strategy use. Winograd and Hare (1988) suggest five elements that can be included in teacher explanations about strategy use: (1) what the strategy is, (2) why the strategy should be learned, (3) how to use the strategy, (4) when and where the strategy is to be learned, and (5) how to evaluate the use of the strategy. Teaching the reader how to monitor successful use of a strategy may be more important than previously thought. A cognitive understanding of what should be done is not enough to guarantee success while reading. The reader must also understand how to apply the use of a given strategy.

The role of teacher explanation

Some of the research that I have done (N. J. Anderson, 1991) indicates that "the most significant finding from these data suggests that there is no single set of processing strategies that significantly contributes to success" (p. 468) in second language reading tasks.

> This seems to indicate that strategic reading is not only a matter of knowing what strategy to use, but also the reader must know how to use a strategy successfully and orchestrate its use with other strategies. It is not sufficient to know about strategies; a reader must also be able to apply them strategically. (Anderson, 1991, pp. 468–469)

Reflect back once again to the analogy of the tapestry. A variety of threads are used in the creation of a beautiful tapestry. Not just one or two, but many. How the threads are woven together will vary from weaver to weaver but all can create a beautiful product. Readers are like weavers. Each can weave the strategies together in a unique way. Good readers use a wide range of strategies and not just a narrow set.

Verbal reports are a tool for the classroom teacher in getting readers to verify what they are doing while they are reading. A verbal report is produced when a language learner verbalizes his or her thought processes while completing a given task (Ericsson and Simon, 1984). Readers can listen to the verbal report

Verbal reports

of another reader who has just read the same material, and it is often revealing to hear what other readers have done to get meaning from a passage. Cohen (1990) suggests that as readers verify what strategies they are using they become more aware of the "full array of options open" to them to improve their reading (p. 73).

Metacognitive awareness

As second language readers actively monitor their comprehension processes during reading, they will select strategies to assist in getting at the meaning of what they are reading. Metacognitive awareness of the reading process is perhaps one of the most important skills second language readers can use while reading. This indicates that they are able to verify the strategies they are using. Metacognition is best defined as thinking about thinking. Verbal reports have been used in many second language research designs as a method of getting at the mental processes that second language learners use to understand the language. Verbal reports allow "insight into the dynamic and interactive nature" of the language learning process (MacLean and d'Anglejan, 1986, p. 814). Getting students to think aloud and use verbal reports is a beneficial metacognitive activity. Irwin (1991) states that

> when students think aloud or hear others think aloud, their metacognitive awareness of options for responding to text increases. It can also help them to become aware of how much thinking goes into comprehending a text. (p. 203)

For more information on teaching main idea comprehension see Baumann, 1984

Based on this theoretical input, second language reading teachers can approach the instruction of reading strategies by addressing the following six questions suggested by Winograd and Hare (1988). The six strategy instruction questions are applied to a specific reading skill: Main Idea Comprehension.

1. *What is the strategy?* Being able to identify the main idea is one of the most important reading skills you can develop. It is a skill that you need to apply to the majority of reading contexts.

2. *Why should the strategy be learned?* If the main idea can be identified, comprehension is facilitated by being able to organize the information presented and by being able to distinguish main ideas from supporting ideas and details.

3. *How can the strategy be used?* Read to locate the thesis statement of the passage and the topic sentences of each paragraph. Read quickly, don't worry about the details.

4. *When should the strategy be used?* Main idea comprehension should be used when reading expository passages which contain much new information.

5. *Where should the reader look?* The reader should read the first and last paragraphs of a passage and read the first sentence of each paragraph. Readers should be reminded to ask themselves the following questions: What idea is common to most of the text? What is the idea that relates the parts to the whole? What opinion do all the parts support? What idea do they all explain or describe?

6. *How can you evaluate the use of the strategy?* In the early stages of reading comprehension, open discussions with the reader will be the best method to verify whether the strategy is being used appropriately. The use of verbal think-aloud protocols can facilitate the evaluation of the strategy.

I have used these six questions as a tool for strategy instruction in my own reading classes. I have a transparency with the six questions in my class folder. I use the questions in two ways. First, I prepare a list of strategies that I know I am going to teach during the class. These are usually determined by questionnaires which I have administered and/or comments from the students themselves about what strategies they want to learn. Second, I use the questions on the spur of the moment in class when the context is right for explicit strategy instruction. I have found that some of the best strategy instruction in my class comes when the use of a strategy naturally emerges from the students themselves and is not planned by me. Both forms of instruction, planned and unplanned, have led to effective teaching.

1 *Prepare an overhead transparency of the six questions above. Select a strategy that you know your class needs to discuss. Select an appropriate reading passage that naturally elicits the use of the selected strategy. Talk through the six questions with your class. Allow them to then practice the use of the strategy. Ask the students to evaluate the explicit instruction of the strategy. Record in your Reflective Reading Journal what you have learned from this activity. What have your students learned?*

Paul Hardin provides insights into the techniques he uses with his students to get them to be aware of their reading strategies.

> Strategic learning is the key to student success in any endeavor. I view learning by strategies as the foundation for lifelong learning. Therefore, as with comprehension, strategic instruction has a pivotal role in all areas of my curriculum. It is a skill learned in the aural/oral classes, composition classes, as well as the reading classes. Since listening, speaking, reading, and writing are all integrated and interwoven into each class, the students receive extensive exposure to the "how to" of these communication modes. I impress upon my students that, "This is but one moment of time in your learning experience. Your next moment will find you on your own, with only the 'how to' that we learned together. Your next slice of life will challenge you to take what we have done and apply it to new learning situations. I can't 'teach' you all you need to know to be a successful learner in English, but I can give the strategies to use in other situations so you can learn on your own and continue to learn all your life." This belief is held constant in all interactions with

students. Other adults and peer tutors in the class reinforce this belief by providing strategies to answer the student's questions and not just giving them the answers.

One thing that I have learned from my students' Reading Survey, completed at the beginning of the semester, illustrates a trait found in many second language learners as they tackle text written in English. They approach it from a bottom-up perspective. They feel they must understand and be able to pronounce each word to comprehend. Thus, they spend hours looking up definitions in bilingual dictionaries and trying to "translate" the text, only to become frustrated by words that are misinterpreted by the dictionary or literal translations that have no meaning in English. As I introduce strategies to assist students in reading more effectively and utilize more top-down approaches to reading comprehension, I notice a sense of insecurity in the students. Their security blanket has been lost. They are uncertain about their reading and understanding of the text. They have lost the reassurance of the bilingual dictionary that gave them the "real" meaning and not a "guess" as these new strategies do. No matter how much I model or have the students rehearse in class, once they are on their own, they miss the training wheels and revert to more familiar and comfortable habits. They miss the confirmation and sense of correctness they felt as they translated every word and sentence.

To counter this fear and give them confidence in using strategies, I give them the immediate confirmation during group or individual reading time. As the students read or experience difficulty in the reading assignment, I will have the student "think aloud" and relate his/her thinking processes as he/she tackles the unknown using one of the strategies used in class. I ask the student to identify the strategy and work through the steps to reach a solution. For example, the student is stopped on an unknown word. He/she examines the word to identify word parts, the role the word plays in the sentence and any context clues that might help define the word. Once the student has completed the analysis and given a response, I will immediately confirm or reassure the student that the analysis was correct and that is the meaning of the word. If the student's analysis was not correct, I would step through the procedure with the student. This would be done in all classes to increase the student's confidence in strategic learning. I have found they need that constant reinforcement to revise the old ways and adopt the new. This nurturing will be frequent at the beginning, but taper off as the students become more secure with their reading. I can't be with them in all situations to provide that reassurance. They need to develop that security from within and trust in their problem-solving ability.

These confidence-building activities are conducted in whole class work, small group work, pair work, individual work and homework. For confidence building in comprehension, I will demonstrate reading a paragraph using strategies we have practiced. I will think aloud as I read the title and predict what the topic of the paragraph or selection is. I'll examine vocabulary words and use strategies to understand the meaning of the unknown words and how they relate to the topic. I'll use background knowledge to see what I already know about this topic. I'll go on to examine pictures and graphics to get clues and confirmation that my predictions are accurate or at least close. This process will continue at the group and pair level and the students will follow the formula and reach some kind of consensus on the topic. Then comes the true proof of the pudding—the individual work. The new reading is placed on each desk. The students are reminded to follow the formula they had in group work. I can see the students nervously looking at each other, then their eyes survey the entire page searching everywhere, but focusing nowhere. I sigh and resign myself to once more stepping them through the process. We begin with the title and they complete their analysis and we move on to the next step until once again we have gone through the formula and they have solved the equation. Where they falter is here at the solution level. They have as yet no mechanism to go back and check their work to ensure the solution is accurate. They are once again uncomfortable and uncertain of their work. To build their comfort level with comprehension, I use a backward build-up procedure that takes the students from their analysis back through the reading to locate actual text that verifies what they have predicted. It provides the students with a tool with which to check their work, much as they do in math. I have the students think aloud as they read their summaries and predictions and reference the text location where they obtained the information to determine the topic or key points. This is done with the whole class so all students can experience the process involved. As the student works through these strategies I will confirm his/her conclusions and provide the student with immediate reassurance that he/she has arrived at the correct solution. If the student has ventured down an incorrect path, then as a class we will retrace each step and clarify the point at which the wrong path was taken.This process will take place at the small group level and the pair level where the procedure will be repeated with new readings. The students will read, analyze, write summaries, determine topics, main ideas, supporting ideas, and key concepts and then share these findings with their partners. As this is accomplished the student will justify her/his conclusions by identifying the text location from which the summary was taken. This provides the student with the immediate reassurance that these new techniques do lead to correct solutions.

Classroom work needs to be augmented by homework as well as practice in other regular education classes. To facilitate extensive practice I ask my students to keep a running log of reading done in other classes. As they read their biology assignment (at first a small part of the assignment only) I have them write questions they may have, look ahead and look back to see how the current section ties in with past learning and how it might lead to future sections. I have them list the strategies they employed in the section, and why they used them. Then I will have the students write a summary of the section. In class the students will share their log with the whole class. It is a variation on the theme of thinking aloud. The students will go through the strategies and explain to the class the content and key points of the section. Since most students are taking the same science classes this also allows those students having difficulties to hear discussions about the topic and ask questions to help them better understand the text. They hear from their peers the steps involved in thinking through and managing the text. When not using actual texts I will give the students a reading or have them choose a reading either expository or narrative and ask them to read and keep a running log of the reading. This will be kept in chart form with the following information listed:

Title of reading   Number of pages read   Strategies used   Page verification

At some point in the week the student and I will conference about this assignment and I will choose a strategy and the student will refer to the page noted next to the strategy and then proceed to think aloud as he/she shows me how the strategy was used and how it helped him/her. Also the student will indicate what information or key points was provided by the strategy. This allows another opportunity for the student to check strategies and understand how he/she becomes an empowered reader by using these tools. The goal is always to instill in the student the purpose of strategic learning. Until students see the value and utility to them they will view it as another exercise done to please the teacher and meet course requirements. They must develop the intrinsic motivation to use this reading method or it is put aside at the end of the class and forgotten.

Strategies are continuously being recycled and used in all content areas. This reinforces my initial comments to the class which stress the important role strategic reading plays in life-long learning. The students become comfortable with reading and comprehending in the second language and more importantly, they see the connection between strategic learning and text comprehension in their other classes. They understand the purpose and feel confident using this approach in English just as they had in their first language.

Strategy training

Grabe (1991) provides a caution: "effective strategy training is not a simple or easy matter" (p. 393). He points out that the duration of training, clarity of training procedures, student responsibility, and strategy transfer are variables that influence strategy training results. In spite of these challenges, additional work in ESL strategy training needs to continue.

In addition to these six questions outlined by Winograd and Hare (1988), (What is the strategy? Why should the strategy be used? How can the strategy be used? When should the strategy be used? Where should the reader look? and How can you evaluate the use of the strategy?) allowing readers to become more aware that what they actually do while reading is extremely beneficial, the application of verbal reports to the L2 classroom provides an opportunity for a teaching of metacognitive awareness strategies in all language skills. The following ten steps can be applied in adapting this research tool to the reading classroom. (Anderson and Vandergrift, 1996, p.9)

1. Select a passage to read aloud to the class in which you will demonstrate the think-aloud procedure. Select a passage that you have never read before in order to demonstrate in as natural a fashion as possible what is going on in your own mind while reading.

2. Read aloud while the students follow silently. While reading verbally report what is going on in your mind while you are reading. For fluent readers, you may need to slow down your thinking processes in order to be aware of what you actually do while you read.

3. At the conclusion of your model, encourage the students to add any of their own thoughts that occurred to them during your reading.

4. You may decide to provide additional models for your students so that they can see what is involved in producing a verbal report.

5. Students can then be grouped into pairs or threes and work together to practice thinking aloud. One student in the group can read aloud while the other(s) follow along silently. Students can be encouraged to verbalize their thoughts and the strategies that they are using during the reading.

6. Students who acted as listeners during this activity can be encouraged to add their thoughts to what their classmate has already shared.

7. The activity can also be done in a "reading round robin" format (Irwin, 1991). The class can be given a reading passage and each student is asked to read one sentence at a time and then verbalize what he or she is thinking about. This activity works best if the readers reveal only one line at a time of the reading passage.

8. A "hot seat" activity can also be applied. One student can be asked to read a short passage and think aloud while the others in the class follow along silently.

9. The think-aloud activity can also be applied to regular silent reading periods. Occasionally during a silent reading activity students can be interrupted and asked to verbalize what they are thinking. The verbal report activity can also be implemented by having students stop at certain points and turn to a partner to verbalize their thoughts.

10. Finally, students can be encouraged to practice this activity outside the classroom. Davey (1983) has suggested that students be asked to read silently and then complete a checklist to report the kinds of strategies they were implementing during the silent reading session. This can very easily be conducted as a homework assignment.

Through the use of this technique in reading classes students can be taught how to be more aware of what they are doing while they are reading and to see what other readers do when they encounter difficulties. Many of the examples that students come up with during their verbal reports in class provide excellent points of discussion about what good readers do when they read.

In practicing verbal reports in class, the focus can be on getting students to "aim for transfer" (Davey, 1983). The objective is to get students to use this in all their reading activities. The demonstration and practice provide not only a discussion of how to read, but also why and when you would use certain strategies.

O'Malley and Valdez Pierce (1996, pp. 120–121) suggest that teachers prepare a think-aloud checklist and record strategies readers report using as they share their strategies with each other. You might consider modifying this checklist and asking the students themselves to regularly check what strategies they used while reading a section of a passage.

Teachers'
Voices

I used the above techniques in my reading classes to get students to become more aware of their reading strategies and to be able to articulate what those strategies are. The first time I decided to do this I wanted to provide an authentic example for my class. I was preparing for class by reading a section from Andrew Cohen's 1990 book, *Language Learning*. In the book Cohen was discussing the value of getting students to monitor their reading strategies and then to discuss what they did. He indicated that thinking about your reading strategies is not an easy thing to do and does require development of metacognitive ability. He suggested that the readers of his book monitor their reading strategies while reading a passage he had included entitled Chernobyl: The Grim Statistics of Cancer. I thought, what a perfect opportunity! I'll stop reading here, make photocopies of this reading and do a live, authentic demonstration for my class. I didn't realize what a risk I was taking.

Below I have two columns. On the left is the passage, Chernobyl: The Grim Statistics of Cancer. On the right are the things that I said to my class about my reading strategies. Imagine this as a live, spontaneous reading and verbalization of my reading strategies.

The Passage	Verbalization of My Reading Strategies
Chernobyl: The Grim Statistics of Cancer	(1) Chernobyl. I remember this nuclear disaster. I don't think I followed this story much. This should be interesting. Grim statistics. I'm going to learn about how many people died from cancer as a result of the meltdown.
Two American physicists have drawn a rough but grim outline of the spread of cancer that could result from the fallout from Chernobyl.	(2) *Could* is an important word here. The grim statistics may only be projections.

They expect tens or even hundredsof thousands of tumours, and possibly several thousand deaths from cancer during the next 30 years. Experts in the US government's nuclear agencies accept the findings.

(3) *Expect.* Another confirmation that we're not sure here.

(4) Just because a government agency accepts these findings, does that mean I have to?

The estimates have been made by Frank von Hippel of Princeton University and Thomas Cochran of the Natural Resources Defense Council, an environmental group. They calculate the following consequences from all routes of exposure:

■ 2000 to 40 000 cases of thyroid tumours from inhalation of iodine-131. Only a few percent of these tumours will be fatal.

(5) Note: I misread thyroid for typhoid on my initial reading and corrected myself.

■ 10 000 to 25 000 cases of potential thyroid tumours from iodine absorbed from contaminated milk.

(6) I wonder why there are no commas used to separate thousands in these numbers. I wonder if this was written by a Brit.

(7) Oh, notice the spelling of tumours. We spell it tumors. This has to be written by a Brit.

(8) Absorbed from contaminated milk. Oh, I get it. The cows must have eaten grass that was contaminated and that caused the milk to be contaminated.

■ 3500 to 70 000 cases of cancer from all sources of caesium-137. About half might be fatal.

(9) What is caesium-137? I have no idea.

Von Hippel and Cochran will describe their research in the September issue of the Bulletin of Atomic Scientists. "There is a lot of uncertainty in the figures," von Hippel stresses.

(10) *Uncertainty.* Even the experts gathering the numbers are not very confident in these findings.

The calculations start from an estimate of contamination of language and the level and of contamination of the air. The pattern of fallout is derived from models made by Helen ApSimon and Julian Wilson of Imperial College, London

(*New Scientist* 17 July, p. 42) and the Lawrence Livermore National Laboratory in California. When combined with data on population densities and standard coefficients for the amount of radioactivity absorbed by human bodies, a "population dose" can be established. For direct inhalation of iodine-131 via crops and food, it is 50–900 million person-rads; and for caesium-137, it is 5–84 million person-rads.

(11) There is no date given for this publication. I don't remember exactly when all this took place.

(12) What is iodine-131? I don't know.

(13) Caesium-137? I still don't know what that is.

Finally, these dose calculations are multiplied by a "dose-consequence" coefficient, which translates a given dose into a figure for the likely increased incidence of death or tumours.

ApSimon and Wilson calculated that the accident at Chernobyl released 15 to 20 megacuries of iodine-131 and 1 to 2 megacuries of caesium-137. These amounts correspond to 20–25 per cent of the reactor's inventory of these two radionuclides when the accident occurred.

(14) *Megacuries.* What is a megacurie? Mega means big. I wonder if a curie has anything to do with Madame Curie.

Scientists are still tabulating how much radioactivity fell where. The maps drawn by ApSimon and Wilson, unlike those made in the US, take into account weather patterns and rainfall over central and western Europe. Rainfall brings radioactivity down to Earth, increasing contamination.

(15) The rainfall could have contributed to the grass contamination, which would lead to the contamination of the milk.

The measured concentration of caesium-137 in Stockholm averaged about 1 becquerel on 28 April. There were hot spots, however, such as at Simpedvarp, on the Swedish coast about 200 kilometers south of Stockholm, where values of 190 becquerels were reported. For the 200 million people in Eastern and central Europe who were most exposed

(16) *Bequerel.* I'm reading stuff I don't really know about. Iodine-131, caesium-137, megacuries, bequerels. These are all new terms to me. I'm nervous because I'm the teacher and I don't want to look foolish in front of my class. Oh well. Just goes to show you that you can't know everything.

To Chernobyl's cloud of radioactivity, the extra dose would be about the same as that received by the generation of humans exposed to the peak of global fallout from atmospheric nuclear tests during the early 1960s.

If, before the accident, the lifetime risk of cancer in an area was 20 per cent, it would now increase to perhaps 20.005 per cent. The high numbers of tumours and cancers are not a result of heavy doses of radiation, but of the sheer numbers of people exposed to a low dose.

(17) This certainly doesn't look like a significant increase to me. Scientists are so exact in their measurements.

(18) We're getting to the end of this article so this must be the conclusion. Let's see what they have to say.

The moral, perhaps, is that in the aftermath of the accident, governments (who should be concerned about the risk of deaths among entire populations) should have panicked more, while individuals need not have panicked as much as they did. (Cohen, A. D. [1990]. Language Learning, pp. 98–99. Boston: Heinle & Heinle Publishers.)

(19) The public is often guilty of blowing things out of proportion.

(20) I really didn't have to know the meanings of the scientific terms in order to understand this article. The statistics still don't look so grim to me. I'll have to watch and see if in several years from now there is ever a follow-up to these statistics that may confirm or refute what this article suggests.

---

2 *Reread the passage above (only the material in the left-hand column). Record the strategies you used while reading. How are your strategies different from or similar to the strategies reported above?*

---

3 *Review the written record of the think-aloud protocol above. What strategies do you see used? Make a list noting the comment number then compare it with the list below.*

Reading strategy
checklist

Keep in mind that not all readers are going to use the same strategies while reading. That is what I have found makes the use of the verbal report such an exciting classroom tool. Readers in your class can listen to the verbal reports of their classmates and see immediately that there are many different ways of reading and understanding the same text. The background knowledge we each bring to the reading setting makes the orchestration of strategies such an individual process. I believe that it is important for readers to learn this point.

Based on some research that I've conducted (Anderson, 1991), I have developed the following Reading Strategy Checklist. The list is not exhaustive, but it does contain common reading strategies that you might want to consider teaching. I have shared this list with students in my classes as examples of possible strategies that can be used while reading. Sometimes the list has sparked a desire to discuss specific strategies that students are unfamiliar with. I have broken the list of 24 strategies into three different groups: cognitive reading strategies (thinking), metacognitive reading strategies (thinking about your thinking/planning), and compensating reading strategies.

Cognitive Reading Strategies

1. Predicting the content of an upcoming passage or section of the text.

2. Concentrating on grammar to help you understand unfamiliar constructions.

3. Understanding the main idea to help you comprehend the entire reading.

4. Expanding your vocabulary and grammar to help you increase your reading.

5. Guessing the meanings of unfamiliar words or phrases to let you use what you already know about English.

6. Analyzing theme, style, and connections to improve your comprehension.

7. Distinguishing between opinions and facts in your reading.

8. Breaking down larger phrases into smaller parts to help you understand difficult passages.

9. Linking what you know in your first language with words in English.

10. Creating a map or drawing of related ideas to enable you to understand the relationships between words and ideas.

11. Writing a short summary of what you read to help you understand the main ideas.

Metacognitive Reading Strategies

12. Setting goals for yourself to help you improve areas that are important to you.

13. Making lists of relevant vocabulary to prepare for new reading.

14. Working with classmates to help you develop your reading skills.

15. Taking opportunities to practice what you already know to keep your progress steady.

16. Evaluating what you have learned and how well you are doing to help you focus your reading.

Compensating Reading Strategies

17. Relying on what you already know to improve your reading comprehension.

18. Taking notes to help you recall important details.

19. Trying to remember what you understand from a reading to help you develop better comprehension skills.

20. Reviewing the purpose and tone of a reading passage so you can remember more effectively.

21. Picturing scenes in your mind to help you remember and understand your reading.

22. Reviewing key ideas and details to help you remember.

23. Using physical action to help you remember information you have read.

24. Classifying words into meaningful groups to help you remember them more clearly.

---

4 *Monitor your own reading strategies during a 15 minute period of reading. Approximately every 5 minutes, stop and identify the strategies you have used while reading. Record the strategies on a piece of paper.*

---

5 *Take the* Strategy Inventory for Language Learning *(Oxford, 1990, version for English speakers learning a new language, pp. 283-291; ESL version, pp. 293-300). How does this self-inventory help you to be aware of your reading strategies? Record your reactions in your Reflective Reading Journal.*

---

6 *If you currently teach, what are your course goals for reading? How do you approach the teaching of reading strategies in the class? What successes or failures have your experienced doing this?*

---

7 *Observe a reading class. What are the overall reading goals for the course? Does the instructor try to make readers aware of reading strategies? Were there opportunities during the class where explicit instruction on strategies would have been beneficial for the readers?*

8 *Talk to a second language learner about his/her reading strategies. Is he/she aware of what happens during reading? Ask him/her about reading strategies in the first language. Does he/she transfer strategies from reading in the L1 to reading in the L2? Record what you learn in your Reflective Reading Journal.*

9 *As you or your students verbalize reading strategies, do you see how integrated the ACTIVE framework is that we are looking at? Activation of background knowledge. Cultivation of vocabulary. Comprehension skills. Reading Rate. Do any of the issues we have discussed in earlier sections reveal themselves in the think-aloud protocols?*

Brain-based research

For more on brain-based research see Caine & Caine, 1997; Christison, 1997

A relatively new area of research which provides additional insights into language learning is brain-based teaching. The metacognitive strategies play a major role in this research. Caine and Caine (1997) state that

> [r]eflection on one's own processes, what is generally called metacognition, and on parts of what we call active processing is the core of high-level learning, because reflection is how people extract meaning from experience. We now see that metacognitive capacities can themselves be further developed. (p. 21)

Perkins (1995) uses the terms "reflective intelligence" when he refers to metacognitive strategies. He emphasizes that metacognitive strategies can be developed and are, in his thinking, an intelligence. He states:

> [Reflective intelligence involves] coming to know your way around decision making, problem solving, learning with understanding, and other important kinds of thinking. . . . The stuff you get is very diverse—strategies, habits, beliefs, values, and more—but it's all part of knowing your way around. (p. 236)

It may be that the development of the metacognitive strategies can have the greatest impact on the development of second language reading skills.

10 *What is your reaction to the statements above by Caine and Caine and Perkins? Can metacognitive strategies be taught? Would you agree that this is an intelligence as Perkins suggests? Record your ideas in your Reflective Teaching Journal.*

11 *Of all the strategies discussed in this chapter, which may be the most important for you to teach the second language learners you work with? Discuss your ideas with other teachers you work with.*

12 *Visit with a teacher who currently teaches second language learners. Ask what strategies he/she feels are the most important to develop in second language readers. Record the ideas in your Reflective Reading Journal.*

CONCLUDING THOUGHTS

The use of strategies, like each of the elements of the ACTIVE framework, is closely tied into the individual student's motivation for reading and comprehending what she/he has read. We'll discuss this in greater detail in Teaching Strategy 7: Build Motivation. Begin thinking now about what role motivation plays in reading.

At the age of 11 I learned that the sound of the string bass had to be integrated with the sound of the other instruments in the orchestra. Reading strategies are neither taught nor learned in isolation. Second language readers need to remember that strategies are orchestrated based on the purpose of reading and studying. Also, having a variety of instruments in an orchestra enriches the sound. A variety of strategies is needed for effective reading. Learners need to be exposed to that variety and explicitly taught some that they do not know about. Learning how to evaluate the effectiveness of strategy use is an important skill to develop.

Suggested Readings

Two articles and two books may be of interest to those who would like to refine their thinking about reading strategy instruction. First, Carrell, Pharis, and Liberto (1989) report a study designed to teach metacognitive reading strategies. This research needs to be replicated in order to provide second language educators additional input on how to teach learners how to be aware of what they do as they read.

A 1989 article by Carrell, Gajdusek, and Wise ("Metacognitive Strategy Training for ESL Reading") provides a current view of the role of metacognition and second language reading. This article can provide some valuable input to a teacher interested in increasing understanding of the role of metacognition.

Anyone really interested in learning about strategy instruction should investigate Rebecca Oxford's book, *Language Learning Strategies: What Every Teacher Should Know* (1989). The book explains the six areas of language learning strategies that Oxford uses in her Strategy Inventory for Language Learning. The book contains a chapter on each of the six areas and is filled with appropriate applications to second language learners. The subtitle of her book says it all: *What Every Teacher Should Know.*

Finally, an increasing amount of research is being conducted on the brain and how we learn. Renate and Geoffrey Caine (1997) highlight research on the potential of brain-based teaching. This book, *Unleashing the Power of Perceptual Change: The Potential of Brain-based Teaching,* along with others that the Caines have written, will provide insights into teaching and learning strategies that I believe will benefit education.

7

STRATEGY SIX

EVALUATE PROGRESS

I recall a folk song that was made popular in the early seventies by Joni Mitchell entitled, *Both Sides Now.* The chorus goes: "I've looked at clouds from both sides now, from up and down and still somehow it's clouds' illusions I recall; I really don't know clouds at all."

I have done quite a bit of traveling during the past few years. I have traveled to South Africa via Europe; to Morocco, Costa Rica, Honduras, Panama; and to several locations within the United States. I have been fascinated with the clouds. I recall a trip I was making to Seattle, Washington. As I sat on the ground at the airport it was dark and somewhat dreary. The flight was delayed because of the storm clouds. As we took off for that flight, once we did get above the storm clouds the sky was blue, the sun was bright! I was amazed at the different perspective I had when I was on the other side of the clouds.

As I have watched the clouds from both sides I have been impressed at how different they can be, and how the environment greatly influences what they look like from the plane and on the ground.

I grew up in the West along the western side of the Rockies. The mountains were like a blockade for the clouds. When clouds blew in they would often stay around for awhile. That is not the case in Ohio where I have also lived. The wind can blow heavy banks of clouds across the sky. There is nothing to slow them down.

From an airplane I have seen a rolling floor of clouds. It is always strange to me to fly "through the floor" and have it suddenly become the ceiling. The sun can be bright on one side and it can be dark on the other.

As you descend through the clouds it is often difficult to get your bearings. You can catch glimpses of the ground and see some things that look recognizable and then you can be immersed in the clouds again and not see anything.

I was just reading the other day about research conducted on Air Force pilots who become disoriented and don't know it. They can fly into a bank of clouds and come out upside down. Other pilots can enter the clouds and always maintain the plane in an upright position.

On another flight to Seattle, Washington, as we approached our destination I noticed a floor of thick, heavy clouds. I knew it must be dark and stormy on the ground. The pilot called our attention to the tip of Mount Rainier. It was absolutely beautiful to see the snowcapped tip of this grand mountain peak poking up through the floor of clouds. That's all we could see off in the distance.

On a flight into Morocco I was amazed to see the floor of clouds almost disappear as we approached Casablanca. I could see the deep blue Atlantic Ocean along the dark brown landscape of Morocco. What a beautiful perspective.

I have often been aware of the fact that from above I get a very different perspective of things on the ground. I can't see the chipped paint on the houses and barns. I can't see the leaves on the trees. I can't see the animal life making their homes in the forests. The big picture really is different.

Just as the words to Joni Mitchell's song indicate, I really don't know clouds, at all.

Recording progress

Just as I have seen both sides of the clouds and really don't know them, I also feel at times that I really don't know evaluation at all. But the analogy of the clouds has been helpful as I have considered the role of evaluation in second language reading.

We need to have two perspectives of evaluation of reading: the big picture and the small details. We need to be able to step back from our work with the students to see a global measure of progress and improvement. We also must have tools for allowing us to look up close at strengths and weaknesses that our students have.

Reading progress records can be effectively utilized by the teacher to assist readers in keeping track of their progress. Recording progress can become an effective tool in motivating readers to continue to improve. Stoller (1986) points out that making progress charts and graphs can facilitate reading improvement and is a "critical aspect of the instructor's responsibilities" (p. 55).

Assessing growth and development in reading skills from both a formal and an informal perspective is often a concern for reading instructors as well as materials developers. The formal evaluation is what the teacher keeps and records. Informal evaluation may not be recorded on paper but is information that many experienced teachers can tell you about individual readers in their classes.

Both quantitative and qualitative assessment activities can be included in reading lesson plans and curricula. Quantitative assessment will include information from placement tests, in-class reading quizzes, and final examinations. Qualitative information can include student responses to questionnaires about reading strategies, teacher observations during in-class reading tasks, and verbal reports from students regarding their cognitive processes during reading. Both of these forms of assessment give the teacher a close-up view of reading ability. Such materials can have a tremendous impact on reading instruction if there is a healthy balance of both types of assessment activities to evaluate progress.

Paul Hardin gives us some background on one way he uses surveys to get an overview of the readers' practices so he can better meet the needs of the readers he works with.

I have been teaching ESL for 22 years in Clover Park School District. I have taught grades K–12. I have coordinated the K–12 program for the district for 18 years. I am currently teaching full time at the high school level. I feel it is important for the readers to understand the population we serve in the high school program. In our school district, Korean is the largest group, followed by Spanish, Philippine language groups, Vietnamese, and various Pacific Island groups. The level of first language needing literacy encompasses a span from pre-literate to grade level and above literacy. Due to scheduling difficulties, various levels of first language literacy can be found in all reading sections. Sociocultural contexts of learning to read vary greatly among the language groups served. These variables plus the ever-present uncertainty of the adolescents' emotional state of being, create an educational environment that demands diverse and creative instructional techniques as well as nurturing guidance.

In view of the unpredictability of my teaching situation, I will discuss each event in reading with the underlying assumption that any approach or strategy used in the classroom is based on the needs and developmental level of the whole student. To achieve this level of understanding of each student I begin each semester with an individual Reading Inventory for each student. In this inventory students answer questions about their reading materials, amount of reading done each day or each week, reason for reading, as young children did they like to have their parents read to them, what was their favorite book or oral story from parents, did anyone in their family read to them in English as a child, frustrations and difficulties they have in reading in the first or second language, how they would like to improve their reading, etc. Two inventories are done, one in English to understand their view of reading in English and a second done in the first language to establish a baseline of first language reading and sociocultural values.

To augment this picture of their reading history, a second academic background survey is given to each student. This survey attempts to develop a view of the student in previous learning environments. The students answer questions about successes and difficulties in other schools, what they feel are their strong points and weak points in study skills and what their immediate and future goals are in terms of continuing on in school or entering the job market. With this information I can develop a program that takes into account what the students' views on reading are and how they feel they have done academically in the past.

I know in one semester or even one year, I will not be able to provide them with learning experiences that will bring them to the level of their native English speaking peers in vocabulary or any other area of reading. I focus my energy, and that of my students, on strategic learning. I develop lessons that will provide the students with the skills to be lifelong learners and to continue the learning process after they leave my class for the day and forever.

Reading log

F

ive classroom record-keeping procedures can be used by teachers for qualitative and quantitative evaluation. The first four provide a close-up view of readers strengths and weaknesses while the fifth is a more global, big-picture step to evaluation.

First, a reading log provides readers a mechanism of accountability to record what they are reading each day. I encourage students to read for at least 30 minutes outside of class each day and record what they are reading. Another way that this reading log has proven useful is to have students record everything they read during the day and how much time they spend reading. Students are often surprised at how much of their day is spent in reading activities. The log does not require the readers to provide a detailed description of their comprehension of what has been read. Some teachers implement a reading log in which the readers must summarize what they have read and/or ask questions to the teacher. Used in this fashion, the reading log can become a tool for teaching for comprehension.

A sample format that I use for the reading log is presented in Figure 7.1.

Figure 7.1: **Reading Log**

Name _____

Date   Reading Time   Reading Material   Comments

_____

_____

_____

Rate and comprehension graphs

Second, reading rate graphs are kept to mark improvement in reading rate. Likewise, a graph of reading comprehension scores can be kept. These two graphs become useful tools for the students to use in setting individual goals. Figures 7.2 and 7.3 provide examples of the rate and comprehension graphs that I use in my classes.

These charts are especially useful to track student progress in reading rate and reading comprehension improvement. I use these charts on a weekly basis by having the students complete a timed reading of 1,000 words and answer 10 multiple choice comprehension questions. The reading passages in Fry (1975) are 1,000 words in length as are also chapter readings in Anderson (1996). Students use the charts to record their reading rate and comprehension score on these weekly activities. I collect the scores from the students and compute a class average for reading rate and comprehension and share with the class after each week's timed reading. The reading rate chart could be modified to fit the length of the passages being read. For example, the reading passages in Spargo and Williston (1980) contain reading passages of 400 words in length. The rate column could be modified to reflect this difference in length of reading material.

Reading rate record

Next, a reading rate record is a tool for readers to calculate reading rate during extended reading periods. This record allows the teacher, as well as the students, to monitor reading rate. For this record the reader multiplies the number of pages read by the average number of words per page. This gives the total

Figure 7.2: **Reading Rate**

TIME (minutes)	1	2	3	4	5	6	7	8	RATE (wpm)
1:00									1000
1:15									800
1:30									667
1:45									571
2:00									500
2:15									444
2:30									400
2:45									364
3:00									333
3:15									308
3:30									286
3:45									267
4:00									250
4:15									235
4:30									222
4:45									211
5:00									200
5:15									190
5:30									182
5:45									174
6:00									167
6:15									160
6:30									154
6:45									148
7:00									143
7:15									138
7:30									133
7:45									129
8:00									125
8:15									121
8:30									118
8:45									114
9:00									111
9:15									108
9:30									105
9:45									103
10:00									100

number of words read, which is divided by the number of minutes spent reading to result in the approximate number of words read per minute.

A simple formula for calculating the average number of words per page is to use the following 4 steps:

1. Count every word on the first five lines of text.

2. Divide the sum in #1 above by 5. This gives you the average number of words per line of text.

3. Count every line on the page.

4. Multiple the total number of lines per page (#3 above) by the average number of words per line (#2 above). This results in the average number of words per page.

Figure 7.3: **Comprehension**

Score	1	2	3	4	5	6	7	8	%
10									100
9									90
8									80
7									70
6									60
5									50
4									40
3									30
2									20
1									10
0									0

Repeated reading record

Fourth, a record of repeated reading practice is a tool in helping individual readers set goals for reading rate improvement and also a tool helping readers see their progress. This particular record is used in conjunction with repeated readings. Figure 7.4 provides a sample reading rate record that I use in my classes.

Figure 7.4: **Reading Rate Record**

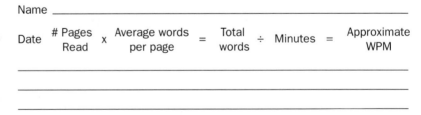

Finally, reading portfolios allow the teacher to see progress over a period of time and to get a better idea of global reading issues. Reading portfolios are excellent tools for allowing the reading teacher to step back and look at big picture issues. O'Malley and Valdez Pierce (1996) indicate that "[p]ortfolio assessment means purposeful selection of specific samples of student work based on student reflection and teacher observations that represent progress" (p. 127). They provide a useful set of eight steps which teachers can follow in preparing portfolio assessments:

1. Specifying purpose
2. Using assessment information
3. Identifying portfolio type
4. Matching contents to purpose
5. Recording student progress
6. Getting students involved
7. Managing time
8. Communication results

Several useful items which could be included in a reading portfolio include:

- Miscue analysis
- Individual reading inventory
- Anecdotal records
- Cloze tests
- Lists of books read
- Sample reading passages
- Checklists/rating scales

The thing that teachers must watch for is multiple opportunities to examine what readers are doing and to document it in some format so that it can be used as a tool to evaluate progress. We need both perspectives: global and close up.

---

1 *Review the reading assessment suggestions in O'Malley and Valdez Pierce (1996) on pages 93–133. What ideas do you get there that help you formulate ideas for a reading portfolio? Record your ideas in your Reflective Reading Journal.*

---

2 *A variety of web pages are available that discuss portfolio assessment. At the date of printing this book, the following web pages were active. Look at these web addresses and review the information they present on portfolio assessment. What ideas do you get here that may help you with your ESL/EFL readers? Record your ideas in your Reflective Reading Journal.*

- http://www.cse.ucla.edu
- http://rgfn.epcc.edu/programs/trainer/www/central/portfolio.htm
- http://www.uncg.edu/~ericcas2/assessment/diga10.html

Dawn shares some insights that have been useful to her in formulating her philosophy of the role that evaluation plays in her reading class.

I use a lot of reading inventories. I get the students to just check off strategies they may be using. I ask them, what are you understanding? What aren't you understanding?

I haven't used portfolios and I haven't come across many ways of using them in a reading class.

I have given my class a reading interest survey. I just gave them another one to check to see if they are reading anything different now. Today we're going to talk about what they enjoy reading in terms of outside reading and in-class reading.

In one class I taught I asked them to keep a reading log. With this current class I didn't do it this time. The feedback was negative. The students saw it as a real chore. I worried that it was detracting from the reading. I would use it again, but I would have to evaluate how I am using it and maybe make it easier for the students. Maybe I could make a checklist. I told them that I wasn't looking at their grammar or writing but I could tell that they had spent a lot of time on the log. Some had written in pencil and had several erase marks. Perhaps I need to restructure the task so that they are not spending so much time writing.

I do a lot of interviews. I see my students for a lot of time outside of class. I think this is just my personal style of teaching. I know that some teachers only see their students at mid-quarter. Some students come to see me weekly.

Some students have so many outside factors affecting their performance. This affects how I look at them. Some students have roommate problems. One student came to see me about problems she was having in an art class. She felt the teacher was ridiculing her in front of the other students. This was affecting her whole demeanor in class and she was frequently on the verge of tears. I get quite involved in students' lives. If they are not handing things in on time it's good to know why and what factors outside of class are influencing their lives. I believe that it helps to know a lot about the students, but don't push if they don't want to tell you.

I have two Russian students. It is very interesting because I have never dealt with anyone from Russia before. I made assumptions about these students before going into class, making comparisons with Polish students I have taught before who were very warm. These guys are very cold. I should have thought of this before. They have just left Siberia. They've never been outside of Siberia. They are 18 years old. I think they were shell-shocked for the first five weeks. They would say nothing in class. I called them in a few times and asked how they thought they were progressing. They wouldn't make eye contact. This was just their way of dealing with their professors. Their behavior started to change at mid-quarter. The down side of it is that I get a lot of students coming to see me about other teachers. It can become problematic. I really think that it is very valuable to get to know the students well. Students are willing to share that they don't understand. They come with things from their other classes. They don't feel comfortable with their other teachers. Sometimes I think they feel too comfortable with me.

I don't do a lot of testing. If I do it's on a topic that we've already discussed. I don't like them going into tests cold.

I do a lot of group work and evaluate them in groups. I think this is helpful to know the students quite well. I know who doesn't like working with whom. There is no point to pushing them into pair work with someone they don't get along with.

I did think-aloud protocols with my more advanced reading class as they were actually reading. It was difficult for them. It was difficult for me to model in class. It really challenged their assumptions about me as a teacher. I asked the students to bring something in from their majors. One student from chemical engineering brought in a reading. I made a transparency of the text and used it in class. I told them that this was an unseen text and I modeled reading it with them. Some students were shocked that I could read something in English and understand only about 60–70 percent of it. Some thought I didn't understand. Some students have a blind faith that you as a teacher can explain anything. It's difficult for native speakers to do and so I don't think this is a good thing for non-native speakers to do. It interrupts the flow of their reading and they can't remember what they have read. They are sometimes spending so much time thinking about what they are going to say.

I have found it helpful to put them into groups of three. The first would read a paragraph and then stop and share with the other two what they had read. That worked well in a strategy share. If they don't understand something one student in the group can often help them by using the text to point out what they have done to understand.

With the skill of inference, for example, they tell me that they know what they did but they can't explain it to me. I don't want to prompt them into things they haven't done. I often do that and they simply agree with me when perhaps that is not what they have really done. It's difficult to get them to think about their strategies.

---

3 *What type of self-assessment tasks do you think are appropriate for ESL/ EFL readers to participate in? Do you believe that level of language proficiency would make a difference in the type of task you ask readers to self-evaluate? Why/why not?*

4 *If you are teaching reading in an ESL/EFL class, prepare a checklist of reading skills that you could use as an informal check of readers' progress. The checklist could be one which could be used over the course of a term and could guide lesson planning.*

5 *Observe a class in which some reading instruction takes place and watch what the readers are doing and saying about their own reading skills. If you were the teacher of such a class, how could you use this observational information as an evaluation tool?*

6 *Prepare a reading interest survey for a group of second language readers. How could information from this survey help you as a teacher to evaluate a class?*

7 *Review the Reflective Journal entries you have been keeping while reading this book. What do you learn about yourself as a reader from these entries? Would a similar assignment for the ESL/EFL readers you are working with provide them with evaluative feedback on their reading?*

Teachers'
Voices

Carolyn tells us about the techniques she has found effective as a reading teacher to evaluate the progress of her Pre K–12 students:

> I like to use a variety of progress records to evaluate student progress: self evaluations, observation checklists, reading logs, and reading journals. The student self evaluations have a variety of questions on what they liked or what caused them difficulty. I also like to add a section called, "When I don't understand." It looks like this:

When I don't understand:	A word	A Phrase	A Sentence
use context clues			
read back			
read ahead			
look it up			
ask someone			
skip it and read on			

For the reading log, I create a chart for students to keep in their notebooks. I put clip art at the top of the categories as a visualization of what the columns are asking in print. I have them keep track of when, where, and what they read, what was their purpose for reading, how long they read, and what one thing they learned. This way students can not only track their progress but also, the teacher and the students have a great source of data that they can analyze for patterns. I've used this reading chart with elementary and secondary students. One teacher in my school district has created a reading chart that is networked in the computer lab. He checks his students' progress by going on the computer every two to three weeks. Students share their progress and data with each other.

I also like to use reading logs where they discuss what they've read with me in an informal way. This is a very nonthreatening open dialogue. I enjoy reading their questions or comments in this format rather than in the archaic "book report." For beginning readers, this reading log is a combination of pictures from magazines or their drawings with phrases or sentences.

Recall the use of graphic organizers referred to in the section on activating background knowledge and teaching for comprehension. Graphic organizers are another tool that teachers can use for evaluation purposes. Keep in mind that any reading activity or exercise you do in class could be used for evaluation purposes. The challenge is making sure that you are evaluating and not teaching. Recall our discussion in the section on Teaching for Comprehension about teaching and not testing (pp. 37–40)? Now the reverse is true.

Graphic organizers

8 *After teaching a group of students about graphic organizers, introduce a new text and ask the students to create a graphic organizer of their own without your assistance. Would this be a useful entry in a student's reading portfolio to demonstrate improvement in reading skills? Why or why not?*

CONCLUDING THOUGHTS

"I've looked at clouds (evaluation) from both sides now, from up and down and still somehow it's clouds (evaluations) illusions I recall; I really don't know clouds (evaluation) at all."

The ability to look at the reading process from all sides makes it easier to evaluate. Evaluation can allow the learner to examine the issues also. Self-reflection is an important component in the evaluation process. When teachers and learners are looking at growth and development, improvement and weaknesses from as many different sides as possible, a more accurate picture will emerge.

Suggested Readings

Authentic assessment is vital in the second language reading context. O'Malley and Valdez-Pierce (1996) have contributed a valuable text (*Authentic Assessment for English Language Learners*) that suggests how second language teachers can move from standardized forms of testing to more authentic forms of testing. Chapter 5 in their book addresses the area of reading assessment.

Allerson and Grabe (1986) address the topic of reading assessment with standard techniques and activities which teachers should consider using as part of their repertoire of assessment techniques. Their article is called "Reading Assessment."

These are valuable resources for any teacher working to establish a philosophy of how to evaluate reading progress.

8

STRATEGY SEVEN

BUILD MOTIVATION

1 *Pause for a moment and consider what factors motivate you to read. Make a list. Share your list with a colleague. What similarities and differences do you see? How similar do you think your list of motivating factors for reading is with a list you might ask your ESL/EFL students to complete? Record these ideas in your Reflective Reading Journal.*

When I was enrolled at the university as an undergraduate I wouldn't say that I was a particularly strong student. I was involved with several activities. I was married and we were expecting our first child. I had a "degree crisis" and decided to change my major. I was enrolled in a business management degree program but realized that I wasn't as happy as I wanted to be. I reviewed my transcript and realized that I was only 1 or 2 classes shy of completing a non-teaching degree in Spanish. I thought this was great since I could graduate within a semester instead of waiting 2 more years in the business management program. I wasn't sure what I would do with a non-teaching degree in Spanish. I knew I didn't want to teach high school Spanish but I knew that teaching was something that I enjoyed. As I visited with my wife she asked if I had considered the MA in TESL/TEFL program. That would be a program to enter with a non-teaching degree in Spanish that would provide a focus on teaching. I checked out the program and applied. I was accepted. My days in the MA program were perhaps some of the best I had experienced to that point in my life.

After completing my MA degree in Teaching English as a Second/Foreign Language I worked for four years in the intensive English program at the university under a non-renewable contract. During the four years I was teaching I knew that I eventually wanted to get into teacher training and that I would need to get a Ph.D. to do what I really wanted. I applied to only one Ph.D. program and was not accepted. It never crossed my mind that I wouldn't be accepted. That was the school I wanted to attend and I knew I was a good teacher worthy of a degree from that program. I had to do some scrambling to look into other programs. A faculty member pointed me toward the University of Texas at Austin. At this same time, I applied for a position with the Center for Applied Linguistics to work in their field office in Manila, Philippines, as the language testing coordinator for the refugee program. I was accepted at UT and was offered a job with CAL. I ended up taking the position at CAL for 2 years and then enrolling in the Ph.D. program at UT.

I learned from this series of events that motivation and success are not luck. They require careful planning and constant work. I have to be clearly focused on what I want and develop a plan for how I am going to get there. I recognized that I must be motivated in my efforts and in my planning. When I am motivated, my thinking is clearer and my work toward my goal is steady and consistent.

Reading for information and pleasure

Why do people read? This question is central to success in creating materials for a reading class. Two broad, general reasons for reading can be: reading for information and reading for pleasure. When readers read for information they approach the text with the goal of being able to gain new information or to increase their learning. Reading for pleasure provides many readers an opportunity to relax and enjoy the world of books. For both reasons, readers expect to be able to comprehend the material being read and to reach their purposes. Readers will be more motivated to read if the materials they are reading help to meet these broad purposes. When readers have a goal to focus on and are motivated to reach that goal, they will make steady and consistent progress toward it.

Rachel shares an experience she had with two students.

I was teaching a lesson on making predictions to the two middle school students I work with. One of the students appeared to be very bright and the other did not seem to care. The bright student caught on to making predictions after 2–3 examples. The "not so bright" student did not catch on. This boiled down to a lack of motivation on the part of the "not so bright" student. I learned that she was only going to be in school in the U.S. for one quarter. Her parents had already told her that they were not going to worry about her grades. The "bright" student, in addition to being more motivated, was also at a higher level of language proficiency. She wanted to make progress in the development of her language skills and prepare to use her skills in gaining a strong education in the U.S.

Since motivation influences just about every other aspect of second language learning, I suspect it influences reading performance as well. Quite simply, if a student is not motivated to read she will not read.

First and foremost, the reader must be interested in what she's reading, otherwise there is no impetus whatsoever. The ESL reading teacher should do his best to discover his student's interests so he can teach via something his students appreciate and enjoy.

Second, readings must be chosen with the student's reading proficiency in mind—it should neither be too easy nor too difficult. What the student reads can, in and of itself, instill motivation.

The reading can't be so difficult that the reader gets frustrated and gives up, nor can it be so easy that the student becomes bored and apathetic. Yet it must be challenging. A sense of accomplishment and satisfaction can be more motivating in the long run, though.

I think you can increase motivation by having students keep a reading log, keep track of their reading rates, do build-up exercises, etc. Anything that lets the student see her progress. As long as there are rewards (increased reading rates and comprehension), as long as obtaining the rewards is challenging and not boring or frustrating, I think there will be motivation.

Dawn reacts to the concept of motivation, linking it back to concepts discussed earlier, like increasing reading rate.

I think using a variety of instructional techniques is influencing the motivation of my students. I often ask myself, is any of this spilling over to their reading outside of class?

The students who are reading academic texts tell me that it's taking less time to read the academic texts and they're understanding more. I have students keep a list of what they are reading outside of class. When I met with each one recently I asked how they were doing and they said they are understanding more. They indicated that they are still having problems with vocabulary. Their problems are not something that I'm worried about because they have the skills to deal with it.

I have a science major in this class. Nothing we look at interests him. I have him bring in material from his field of study to practice reading rate. He reads the material quickly and tells me that he is understanding more now than earlier.

I also have some material scanned into the computer for practice in increasing reading rate. Materials that the students bring in from their fields of study allow them to practice reading rate development in subjects that are of interest to them. Overall this influences their motivation.

---

2 *In what ways do you believe that motivation influences reading performance? How could you increase the motivation of readers in your classes? Record your ideas in your Reflective Reading Journal.*

Irwin (1991) summarizes work by Dulin (1978) in which a model for motivation is proposed. The model suggests:

$$\text{MOTIVATION} = \frac{\text{EXPECTED REWARD}}{\text{EXPECTED EFFORT}}$$

The role of motivation

Irwin emphasizes that "motivation can be increased by increasing the expected reward or by decreasing the expected effort. The greatest amount of motivation would result from doing both of these things" (p. 145). She then provides suggestions for increasing the expected rewards and decreasing the expected efforts. These suggestions are provided in Table 8.1. Several of the items listed under "decreasing expected effort" have been discussed within the ACTIVE reading framework above.

Table 8.1: Selected Sample Procedures for Increasing Motivation

Increasing Expected Reward	Decreasing Expected Effort
Provide regular praise	Provide background information
Provide interesting activities	Give specific purpose
Write fair tests	Preview assignment
Provide high-success tasks	Preview vocabulary
Involve students in purpose setting	Discuss reading strategies
Involve students in questioning	Use high-success materials
Use meaningful reading tasks	Divide long chapters into shorter assignments
Give students choices	

Irwin, J. W. (1991). Teaching Reading Comprehension Processes, *second edition, p. 145. Englewood Cliffs, NJ: Prentice Hall.*

3 *What is your reaction to the information presented in Table 8.1? What specific things could you do to decrease the expected effort in your reading classes? How can you increase the expected reward? Record your ideas in your Reflective Reading Journal.*

Irwin and Baker (1989) provide ten suggestions for motivating students on specific assignments (Table 8.2).

Table 8.2: General Suggestions for Motivation on Specific Assignments

1. Never give a reading assignment without thinking about how to motivate students.

2. Never present reading as a chore or a punishment.

3. As much as possible, increase the reward and decrease the effort (see Table 8.1).

4. Give students some control over what and why they read.

5. Follow reading assignments with activities that allow the students to use what they learned while reading.

6. Make all reading assignments relevant, meaningful, and useful by giving the students an interesting purpose for reading.

7. When possible, use reading materials that are related to the students' interests.

8. When possible, show the students how the material might be useful to them in the future.

9. Show that you are also interested in the material.

10. Make sure that each student has a chance to succeed.

Irwin, J. W., and Baker, I. (1989). Promoting Active Reading Comprehension Strategies, p. 58. Englewood Cliffs, NJ: Prentice Hall.

4 *Have you tried any of the ideas listed above in Table 8.2? What has worked for you in motivating your readers? What hasn't worked? Based on your experiences as an ESL/EFL teacher, is there something that you would add to the list? Record your ideas in your Reflective Reading Journal.*

If reading teachers continually keep in mind that reading is done with a purpose and thus direct students in meaningful purposes, and if reading materials are chosen accordingly, the motivation to read and improve reading skills will be present.

The role of the teacher is integral to the success of second language readers. Teachers should view themselves as facilitators helping each reader discover what works best. The ACTIVE reading framework provides a pedagogical tool for the teacher to integrate the principles from reading theory with classroom practice. This integration can lead to more effective reading instruction in the second language classroom.

A tool that teachers can use in the classroom to measure motivation is a questionnaire. As part of a dissertation I supervised, Wengpeng Zhang developed a nice questionnaire that is appropriate for use in examining motivation and strategy issues in the classroom. Look at her questionnaire:

The role of the teacher

Inventory of Motivation for Language Learning (IMLL)

Response Scale

1: Strongly Disagree

2: Disagree

3: Are Neutral

4: Agree

5: Strongly Agree

Inventory of Motivation for Language Learning

Section 1

1. English is a very difficult language for me to learn.

2. I am confident that I can do an excellent job on English assignments and tests.

3. I believe that I understand what is taught in my English class.

4. I have no confidence in learning English.

5. I have a special aptitude for learning foreign languages.

6. I expect I can do very well in English.

7. I believe that my study skills are excellent.

8. I have no idea about how to learn English well.

9. I am certain that I can master the language skills taught in English class.

10. I feel uneasy and lack confidence when speaking English.

11. Considering the degree of course difficulty, the teacher, and my own capabilities, I believe that I can learn English well.

12. I am not good at learning English.

13. I am sure that I understand the most difficult part of the learning materials in my English course.

14. Learning English is important for me because it will make me a more knowledgeable person.

15. Learning English is important for me, for a command of English may provide me better opportunities to get a good job.

16. I learn English because I have to.

17. I study English to learn about other cultures and people better.

18. English is useless, it shouldn't be a compulsory course.

19. Learning English is a waste of time for me.

20. I should not be forced to learn English.

21. I am very interested in the subject matter of English.

22. I believe that what I learn in English class can be used in my future studies of other subjects.

23. I learn English so that I can pass the exams for university.

24. Learning English is important for me because I plan to study abroad in the future, if it is possible.

25. Learning English is boring.

26. I enjoy learning English very much.

27. Learning English is important for me because a command of English may help raise my social status.

28. I take English only because it's a compulsory course.

29. I learn English because I want to express myself and introduce my culture to foreigners.

30. I am not motivated to learn English at all.

31. I believe that I study English more than any of my classmates do.

32. I always actively think about what I learn in my English class.

33. In my English class, I volunteer answers as much as possible.

34. Compared to other subjects, I put the least effort into English.

35. After I get back my English homework, I read the teacher's comments carefully and rewrite the part where I made errors.

36. If it's for me to decide, I would not do any English homework.

37. After graduation, if I do not go to college, I will stop learning English immediately.

38. After graduation, if I do not go to college, I will keep on learning English until I master it well.

39. If I had opportunities to speak English outside of school, I would speak as much as possible.

40. If the local TV station has an English program, I will watch it as much as possible.

41. I prefer English texts that can provoke my curiosity, even if they are more difficult.

42. Even if I did poorly in an English test, I could learn something from my errors.

43. In learning English, I prefer competition to cooperation.

44. If I am asked to choose between two English reading assignments, one is challenging and interesting, the other is easy but boring, I will definitely choose the challenging one.

Section 2

45. What is the major reason for one's success in a foreign language test?

    1. He's smart

    2. He works hard

    3. He has good luck

    4. The test is easy

    5. He has a good teacher

46. How important do you think intelligence is for learning English?

    1. Not important at all
    2. Not important
    3. Medium
    4. Important
    5. Very important

47. How important do you think learning strategies are for learning English?

    1. Not important at all
    2. Not important
    3. Somewhat important
    4. Important
    5. Very important

48. How important do you think attitude and motivation are for learning English?

    1. Not important at all
    2. Not important
    3. Somewhat important
    4. Important
    5. Very important

49. What do you think of your gains in the English course as compared with those from the other courses?

    1. Very little
    2. Little
    3. Moderate
    4. Much
    5. Very much

50. What do you think of your achievement in English as compared with the other students in your class?

    1. Very poor
    2. Poor
    3. Average
    4. Good
    5. Excellent

51. What other motives, thoughts and feelings do you have regarding learning English, which are not included in the statements above?

© 1995, Wenpeng Zhang

5 *Administer the above questionnaire to a student or group of students. Review the responses with the student(s). What do you learn about motivation and language learning? Record your ideas in your Reflective Reading Journal.*

6 *Identify what motivates you. Prepare a lesson plan for an ESL/EFL reading class in which your objective is to discuss the role of motivation. How would you address this important topic with your class? Record your ideas in your Reflective Reading Journal.*

7 *Interview an ESL/EFL teacher about the role of motivation in the classroom. What factors does this teacher identify as having the greatest impact on student motivation? Record the ideas in your Reflective Reading Journal.*

Paul Hardin shares with us his insights on the role that motivation plays in second language reading with the students he works with.

> As I look back at my comments on the areas of vocabulary, comprehension and strategies, I realize that I view them all as critical components to communication. Without vocabulary, comprehension is impeded. Without comprehension there is limited communication, or miscommunication. Without strategies, reading becomes a chore instead of enjoyment. Without motivation all of the above become null and void. If motivation is low, then all the wonderful lessons in the world will not change a student into a reader. Without that internal drive, the student becomes a vehicle in neutral, spinning his/her wheels, but going nowhere. How do we shift that student into gear? How do we move from neutral to drive and provide that student with the internal desire to take the learning and run? That is the troubling question I face each time I enter the classroom.
>
> The solution is at times evasive, but the cause is usually apparent: students from backgrounds that view education as a low priority or no priority for women. Students from backgrounds of poverty that necessitate that the student work after school, weekends, or instead of school to supplement the family income. Students living on their own who must work to survive. Students torn from the security of their homeland to attend school in a new land because the parents feel it will be better for the student and the family. Students from dysfunctional families that experience or see abuse daily. Students in their early teens who are still children, but are asked to look into the future to pick a career. Students who feel they are not good enough for college or university. Students who know from an early age that even if they are "allowed" to stay in school until they graduate, their education will end because they have no resources for college and must work to support themselves or their family.

These are but a few of the obstacles that students face as they attempt to find purpose in learning. The desire to learn is there, but the reality of these mountains which must be climbed is overwhelming to many. It becomes my task to show the students the path of least resistance. This must be accomplished before any lessons are introduced. The students must be able to visualize that path and see that there is safe passage through the obstacle course. To begin this process I go back to the background survey that each student completed at the beginning of the semester. I learn all I can about each student and the situation(s) that brought him or her to my class. I strive to understand them as students and people. We talk about their goals for school and after graduation. As each obstacle is presented by a student as to why he/she can't go on to college or why they always fail at school, I counter with a reason why they can accomplish that goal. I try from the very beginning to instill confidence in them. To formalize this concept a contract between the student and myself is written and signed by both. In this contract I agree to provide them with the skills they need to accomplish their goals for this semester. They agree to believe they can succeed if they work toward these goals. This is a start. It does not provide instant motivation; for some students it is just another promise they will make and break. For some it is another promise from an adult that will be broken.

My next task is to provide lessons that are relevant to the students' goals and interests. In each lesson they must see its importance to them and feel confident when they take on the task individually. Confidence building is critical at this point. The students may see the value to them and their contract, but if they feel uncomfortable with the task when they are on their own, the desire to continue will fade.

I use activities throughout the semester to make students feel comfortable in the class. With this comfort and confidence comes the motivation to take risks which in turn leads to learning. To make students more aware of each other as they start a new semester, I have the students take part in an awareness building exercise. I ask the students to form a circle and identify someone with which they feel they have nothing in common. This person's identity remains secret as the activity proceeds. I will then have each corner of the room identified with a letter (A, B, C, D). In this activity I ask the students to always know where their secret person is. I then ask the students questions about various subjects and the students go to the appropriate corner based on their likes, dislikes or beliefs. Some of the questions are:

If you like dogs as pets, go to letter A. If you like cats as pets, go to letter B. If you don't like any pets, go to letter C. Look around and quietly find your secret person. Note mentally with which letter he/she associates.

If you play an instrument, go to letter B. If you don't play an instrument, go to letter A. If you would like to play an instrument, go to letter C.

After 10–15 questions dealing with a variety of subjects, the students are asked how many were never in a group with their secret person? How many were in a group 2 times? Three times or more? They then begin to see how much they have in common, how others feel about certain subjects. The students no longer feel isolated. They begin to connect and feel comfortable in the class.

Another activity to draw out the students who avoid taking risks by answering or sharing information, is a form of TPR (Total Physical Response). In this activity a question is asked and all who think they know the answer make a fist. The teacher makes sure all students understand that if they have made a fist it is possible that they will be asked to give their answer. Then the teacher asks for a volunteer to answer the question.

The reticent students participate without anxiety. They hear the correct answer and whether their answer was correct or not, they receive immediate feedback and have participated in the activity with no risk taken. The students' comfort and confidence level increase and the fear of participating lessens. The students are more motivated to participate and learn from others.

Allowing the students to respond or demonstrate their understanding using other intelligences is also critical in increasing student motivation. Students may be more comfortable responding through drawing or other fine art modes. Some students will respond through drama or will use movement to respond and demonstrate understanding. Being receptive to alternate learning and intelligence modes will increase the students' comfort and confidence level which leads to motivation.

Changing the structure of the classroom has also been beneficial. Allowing the students to choose topics or themes to be read, encouraging students to express linkages of reading materials to their own life experiences, and relating classroom reading to students' background knowledge reinforce the new learning experience and increase the students' confidence in the learning situation. Choosing materials that relate to the individual interests and goals of the students will increase motivation.

I have found that one of the most effective means of increasing motivation is using instructional methods that teach students how to use strategies to comprehend text material. Strategies provide a purpose for the reading assignment and lessen the effort by increasing success with the text.

8 *Think about what you have just read from Paul. Is his experience similar to or different from yours? Are there any elements of his experience with the role of motivation in the reading class that you want to consider in your own teaching? Record your ideas in your Reflective Reading Journal.*

9 *Develop a secret partner activity like the one Paul describes on pages 108–109. Try it out in your class. What do the students learn from this activity? What do you learn about your students? Record your ideas in your Reflective Reading Journal.*

Motivation and reading rate

Think back to the discussion of Nuttall's model of the vicious cycle in the section on increasing reading rate (page 59). Her virtuous cycle suggests that reading faster encourages the reader to read more. Reading more leads to better comprehension. Better comprehension leads to increased reading rate. The more that one succeeds in reading the more motivated one gets.

10 *Think about all the elements of the pedagogical framework I have shared with you so far: activate prior knowledge, cultivate vocabulary, teach for comprehension, increase reading rate, verify strategies, and evaluate progress. How does your motivation as a teacher influence how these elements would be addressed in the reading class? How does the students' motivation influence how these elements are addressed? What relationships are there between these individual elements and motivation?*

CONCLUDING THOUGHTS

Motivation and success cannot be equated with luck. As we go through life there are often critical moments where it looks as if our plans and desires will not be realized. When we carefully examine our situations and work at maintaining our optimism and look for ways to solve our problems, success will result. This key is held by the individual, not a teacher or a textbook. As reading teachers we should do our part to make sure that the environment lends itself to optimism, but we cannot take the responsibility for self-motivation from the learners. They must decide what they want from the reading class and determine what they need to do to get there. As reading teachers we can then be there to help facilitate the process.

Suggested Readings

I believe that four key articles might be of interest to anyone investigating the role of motivation and language learning. First, a classic by Gardner and Lambert, "Language Attitudes and Language Learning" (1982). This is an excellent place to begin reading to gain additional insights on this topic.

In 1991, Graham Crookes and Richard Schmidt published an article entitled "Motivation: Reopening the Research Agenda." They began to examine the issue of motivation after a few years of silence on the topic.

Dörnyei published two excellent articles in *The Modern Language Journal* in 1994, "Motivation and Motivating in the Foreign Language Classroom" and "Understanding L2 Motivation: On With the Challenge." His treatment of the topic provides valuable insights on understanding motivation and suggests where we need to go in order to better meet teacher and learner needs.

9

STRATEGY EIGHT

PLAN FOR INSTRUCTION AND SELECT APPROPRIATE READING MATERIALS

I have only been ice skating a few times in my life. I have always enjoyed watching the Winter Olympic Games on television and being able to see the ice skaters move across the ice with such skill and such ease. They make it look so easy!

As a child I had a few opportunities to give ice skating a try. There was a pond not far from our home that was used by the community during the winter for ice skating. I remember receiving a pair of inexpensive ice skates one year as a Christmas present. I enjoyed learning how to lace the skates so that my ankles would be adequately supported. I remember how tired I was after the first few minutes of skating. I was having fun and yet at the same time I knew that I was getting tired.

As an adult I accompanied a group of international students on an ice-skating trip. I remember thinking then how easy it was for some of the students to glide across the ice. Others had a more difficult time. I asked one student who seemed to have such a natural ability to give me some pointers. He had a difficult time describing what he was doing. Ice skating seemed to just come naturally to him. Others could give me advice which I then used in assisting some of the students who were having difficulties. On this particular ice-skating trip I remember the great feeling of ease that came to me the longer I skated. One can make remarkable improvement as one practices.

Some reading teachers make teaching look so easy. Some seem to glide through the time and make smooth transitions from one section of a lesson plan into others. I have also observed classes where the teacher seemed to be having difficulties. Just like learning to ice skate, learning to plan for and execute a reading lesson requires practice. With practice and time one can make remarkable improvement.

Let me present some guiding principles that have assisted me in the lesson planning process. Aebersold and Field (1997, pp. 188-191) suggest five factors that influence planning for reading instruction:

- Time
- Progression
- Student groups and cooperative learning
- Variety
- Students' needs, interests, and abilities

Knowing how much time you have to engage in reading and knowing what you have already taught and what you will be teaching are two important factors a teacher can begin focusing on. The decision to involve students in group work and cooperative learning requires careful thought because of the time involved in completing activities of this nature. Variety is a factor that is worth some thought. We want to make sure that readers have a variety in the kinds of texts they read as well as the kinds of skills and strategies that we cover. Finally, consideration of students' needs, interests, and abilities will greatly influence the selection of material. This feature will be addressed later in this chapter.

---

1 *Review the five factors presented by Aebersold and Field. Can you identify other factors that influence your planning for reading instruction? Share these with a colleague. Record them in your Reflective Reading Journal.*

Parts of a
lesson plan

I have been greatly influenced by the Lesson Planning materials in the *Teacher Training Through Video* series (Savage, 1992). Based on the information presented on lesson planning in these materials, I review questions in eight areas when I plan for reading instruction:

1. *Teaching objectives:* What reading skills or strategies do you want the students to be able to use after this lesson?

2. *Materials:* What reading material or additional support material do I need to conduct this lesson? Does the reading material selected allow for the natural use of the skill or strategy I want to focus on during this reading lesson?

3. *Warm-up/Review:* How can I connect today's instruction with previous instruction and/or prepare the class for what is coming?

4. *Introduction to the new lesson:* How can I introduce the purpose of today's instructional objective(s)?

5. *Presentation:* How can I present the reading skill/strategy that I want the students to learn?

6. *Practice*: How can I provide a variety of ways in which the learners can practice the new reading skill/strategy?

7. *Evaluation:* How will I know if/when objective(s) are met?

8. *Application:* How can I involve the students in the reading skill/strategy outside of the classroom?

These questions influence my preparation for the reading class.

---

2 *What questions do you consider when you plan for reading instruction? What similarities are there between your questions and the questions above?*

---

3 *Select a class to observe. Prior to the observation, meet with the teacher and review what he/she plans to teach during the time you will observe. Ask him/her how he/she developed the plan. Is it written out? How detailed is the plan? Then observe the class.*

---

4 *If you completed Investigation 3 (above), conduct a follow-up interview with the teacher after the observation. What changes happened between the plan and reality? What factors influenced the change in the plan? How will the class you observed influence the teacher's preparation for the next class session he/she will conduct with that class?*

One practice I have found very helpful for me as a reading teacher is the self-reflective evaluation following a reading class. Sometimes my self-evaluation is more structured. I find that these more structured sessions with myself occur when a lesson has not gone as I had hoped it would. After a difficult class I will immediately sit down with my lesson plan and make notes of what didn't go well and why I think it didn't go smoothly. I make these notes because I know that I will have the chance to teach the lesson again to a class in the future. It also helps me prepare for the very next class session so that I know how to review and prepare to move forward with them. Most of the time my self-evaluation occurs as I walk from the classroom back to my office. Sometimes just mentally reviewing the success helps me in future lessons.

Self-reflective evaluation

---

5 *Do you self-evaluate following your teaching? How do you conduct these sessions with yourself? Have such self-evaluations benefited your teaching? How? If not, why not?*

Eskey (1986) reminds us that "the first concern of any reading teacher is to find, or create, a body of material that his particular students might find interesting to read, and then to do everything in his power to make it as comprehensible to them as he can" (p. 4). This task is challenging but is often manageable for individual instructors who know the interests of their students. Recall the fifth factor that Aebersold and Field suggest: knowing the students' needs, interests, and abilities. These are essential factors to consider when selecting material to be read in class.

Assessing students' needs and interests

Investigations

6 *If you are currently teaching a reading course, what criteria do you currently use to select a text? List the criteria in your Reflective Reading Journal.*

7 *Which of the following criteria do you use (or think should be used) in selecting appropriate reading material? Record your ideas in your Reflective Reading Journal.*

- the goals and objectives of the course
- the specific needs and interests of the students
- the level recommended by the publisher/author of a textbook
- the reading levels of the students
- whether the texts are fiction or nonfiction
- whether the material is based on a skills approach to reading
- whether the material is based on a strategies approach to reading
- whether the material is authentic
- whether the material has been modified for ESL/EFL learners
- whether the material teaches language structures
- whether the material teaches vocabulary in a natural context
- whether the material is based on academic textbooks

8 *Talk with a teacher who is currently teaching a reading class. What factors does she or he use in selecting appropriate reading material? Record your findings in your Reflective Reading Journal.*

9 *Compare the lists of criteria you have made at this point (criteria you already use, if you are currently teaching, what you think is important, what another reading teacher uses for criteria). Do you see any similarities in your lists? Record your findings in your Reflective Reading Journal.*

Frameworks

**Considerations
for text
evaluation**

Nuttall (1996, pp. 170-176) lists three criteria for evaluating texts for reading development: suitability of context, exploitability, and readability. She suggests areas for consideration for each of these criteria. For suitability of context she reminds reading teachers of two things: finding out what students like and selecting texts for classroom study. Recall the concepts we discussed in the previous chapter on the role of motivation and the selection of texts for classroom reading. Next, Nuttall indicates that exploitability of the text includes the purpose of the reading lesson, integrating reading skills, and stimulating real-life purposes. Finally, in suggesting that readability be a criterion for consideration,

Nuttall recommends that reading teachers assess the student's level, consider how much new vocabulary is introduced in the text, assess the structural difficulty of the passage, and finally calculate the readability level of the material.

In reality, all these factors can influence a reading teacher's decision in selecting the materials and texts to be used in class. A healthy combination of these variables provides the teacher with the information necessary to make an informed decision.

In 1957 E. A. Betts published a book which he titled *Foundations of Reading Instruction*. In this book he outlined some general guidelines for teachers to use in determining if the correct books were being selected for classroom and individual reading instruction. These guidelines published over forty years ago still provide valuable assistance for reading teachers. Betts outlined four levels of reading: basal level, instructional level, frustration level, and capacity level. Let's examine these levels and see how this information may be helpful for a second language reading teacher.

The basal reading level is the independent reading level. The reader should be able to read the material without help from the teacher and should show high interest in it. The reader would achieve 90% comprehension when reading basal level material. It is this level of reading material that I suggest teachers use when beginning work on reading rate development. You do not want the materials to be challenging when trying to improve rate. Also, this is the level of material you might consider using when introducing new reading skills or strategies. Keep in mind that you want the learners to have a successful experience practicing new reading skills so the text should be rather easy at this initial stage. I would also suggest that this be the level of reading difficulty for extensive reading materials. You want the readers to have a fluent reading experience and this can be achieved with basal level reading materials.

Basal reading level

The instructional level is what Betts calls the "teaching level." Readers would achieve 75% reading comprehension when using instructional level materials. This is the level of difficulty you would want when practicing reading skills. After introducing new strategies and having an opportunity to do some practice, the difficulty of the text could be increased to the instructional level to allow for more challenging practice.

Instructional reading level

The frustration level is one that I would think we want to avoid. Betts indicates that reading material at this level is too difficult and frustrates the reader. Comprehension at less than 50% would indicate frustration level materials.

Frustration reading level

The capacity level that Betts suggests is the learner's *listening* level to material read aloud by the teacher. I think that most teachers would agree that comprehension precedes production. Some readers may be able to listen to materials read by a teacher at a level that is higher than their individual reading level.

Capacity level

One application of the Betts framework which I have occasionally used is to encourage students in my classes to go to the library and select a novel to read. I suggest that they might select a book first based on the title. After selecting a book I suggest they open to any page and read. They should raise a finger for each new vocabulary word they encounter. Depending on the length of the page, if they see that they have raised 10 fingers, perhaps the difficulty level of the text is above their current level of reading. They should then select another book and try again. Using Betts' comprehension suggestions above, I suggest that they find a book at the basal or instructional reading levels and avoid books at the frustration level.

10 *Select several books at varying levels of difficulty and apply Betts' suggestions for selecting a book at the right level. Work with a second language reader to see which of the books is at the basal and/or instructional levels. What do you learn from this investigation? Record your ideas in your Reflective Reading Journal.*

Flexible use of textbooks

Over time I have developed a skill for determining the reading passages I use in my classes. What has been an important factor for me is not to let others determine for me what I will use but for me as the teacher to make that decision. In all of the programs I have taught in there has been a prescribed text to be used in the course. This factor will probably be true for the majority of teachers in ESL/EFL programs around the world. I have had the flexibility of selecting the chapters we use in the text and I have had flexibility in selecting the supplemental passages used in the course.

I know some teachers who are given the book and simply follow it step by step from chapter 1 to chapter 10, never giving real thought to the use of the passages. No teacher should ever feel bound to follow a textbook author's way of approaching the material.

11 *Talk with a reading teacher about the materials used in his/her class. What input did he/she have in the selection of the materials? Does he/she have to cover all of the chapters in the text in a prescribed order? What flexibility does the teacher have for selecting which chapters in the book are covered? Does the teacher have the flexibility to supplement the prescribed text? What did you learn from this investigation? Record your ideas in your Reflective Reading Journal.*

The role of authentic materials

Let me address for a moment the issue of authentic materials. Teachers must consider the type of materials that they will use in the reading class. Nuttall (1996) and Wallace (1992) suggest that the selection of authentic text is vital to reading instruction. By authentic texts we often mean that the texts have been written for native speakers of the language and not for second language readers.

I would like to suggest that the focus should be more on the authentic use of material and not so much on the authenticity of the material itself. I know that many times with beginning level learners I have needed to adapt a text to meet the reading level of the class. Somehow I have felt guilty in doing this because I have read so much advice from "the experts" who suggest that we should only use authentic texts. I have arrived at a solution that has allowed me to get rid of the guilt. If I need to adapt material to the reading level of the students, I will. But, I make sure that we are engaged in authentic use of the material. If beginning level readers are engaged in the reading skill or strategy that is the focus of the instructional objective for the class session, then I know that I am building reading skills. If after using a text which I have adapted I find that the readers are not engaged in authentic use of the passage, I consider what additional changes I must make so that the purpose for reading the material is reached. Even though some reading experts suggest avoiding adapted materials, I suggest that you consider the authentic use of the material for the needs of the students you teach.

---

12 *Have you used adapted materials before? Have they been successful? Why or why not? Have you considered the authenticity of the reading task(s) you have engaged the readers in with the adapted material? Can you have authentic tasks with adapted materials? Record your ideas in your Reflective Reading Journal.*

Investigations

Teachers' Voices

I have found that choosing appropriate material can be quite challenging, especially teaching in an IEP program. One problem I face is that the classes are often mixed in terms of students' levels and majors so that I can have a post graduate Education major in the same class as a Sports Administration undergraduate. Obviously these students have very different needs and expectations, and I find that trying to maintain the interest of everyone in the class is often difficult.

One of the first challenges comes with the choice of textbook. I have been lucky enough to teach with some excellent texts, but I have also used others that have been very dull. If you have no control over the book you are given, the best option is to start to build up your own library of supplemental materials. I cut articles from newspapers and a wide variety of magazines. I like to focus on an interesting topic that is in the news and collect several articles related to the same theme from different sources. I then have the students read and compare the articles for content and writing style. I often choose topics that are in the news but are also related to some of the academic disciplines. For example, one quarter I had several science majors in my class and I collected articles about cloning, which was in the news at that time. I also encouraged students to bring in their own articles on the subject. This topic appealed to the science majors but also to the other students who enjoyed participating in the ethical debates that followed the readings. Finding something that appeals to everyone in this way is one of the most difficult tasks instructors are faced with.

Another problem is that many students, particularly at the graduate level, want to focus solely on their academic work. Although I think this is very important, it is also difficult to achieve with a class of 14 different majors. I try to target the students' individual majors particularly in out-of-class work. I achieve this by getting students to select texts from academic journals within their discipline. I then scan the texts into the computer so that the students can practice a wide range of reading activities, such as increasing their reading rate, on academic material.

By choosing their own texts, students have more control over their learning and classes become more individualized. After reading the texts the students complete a written or oral summary of what they have read. This activity works well for students in an IEP program who are frustrated about having to study English and not being able to pursue their major. The negative side is that it often requires a lot of work by the instructor as she/he needs to be familiar with the texts that are chosen by the students. I have read articles on such varied topics as DNA structure and bridge design, and I frequently need the aid of a dictionary to understand them. However on the plus side this has allowed me to see what kind of materials my students will be faced with in their academic classes, and often makes students more realistic about their ability to move immediately into full-time academic study. In addition, it provides students with an opportunity to show off their knowledge as I often ask them to exchange articles and read something from a very different field. I then ask the students to pair up with the original reader and have them explain and discuss the difficult concepts to the rest of the class. By doing this, students get a sense of each others' academic strengths instead of merely perceiving each other as people who have problems with English.

As is true with other ideas presented in this book, the selection of reading materials must be made by the teacher him/herself. I cannot tell you what factors you must use to determine exactly what will work for you and your students. Basically, I would urge you to use whatever materials you can to get your students to read more. I've used articles from hair style magazines and car magazines in addition to the usual sources such as textbooks and journal articles. Students should be encouraged to see reading in English not only as an academic experience but also as a source of pleasure.

13 *Do you follow the textbook activities exactly as they are outlined for you in a book? Do you supplement the textbook with additional readings? Do you use authentic readings? Do you use authentic reading tasks? Record your responses in your Reflective Reading Journal.*

Let's now look at some input from Carolyn. Her Pre-K–12 experience has led to her development of criteria she uses for selecting appropriate reading materials for second language learners.

> I always suggest to teachers and staff that they choose a variety
> of materials for their ESL students. Materials need to be interesting
> and motivating for students to want to read them. We have comic
> books of the classics, chapter books from Steck Vaughn, classic
> books from the "Dollar Stores," SRA Reading Laboratory, biographies, nonfiction reading in science, and much more. All materials
> need to be challenging but at levels that students can succeed at
> reading. Teachers create a reading library that will include not
> only a variety of materials but materials at a variety of levels.
> At the secondary level the caution is to make sure that the materials
> are appropriate to reading and age levels. I once had a teacher who
> planned to do an entire lesson on the reading skill of prediction
> using Dr. Seuss' "Hand, Hand, Finger, Thumb" for 8th grade

students. We need to be very aware of the appropriateness of materials for our students. Yes, this book might have been at the correct reading level, but it was not motivating or appropriate for the age of these students. Publishers are doing a wonderful job at developing challenging, fun, exciting reading materials for our secondary school students.

At the elementary level, new chapter books, nonfiction readings on science, and biographies are coming out for our younger students to read and enjoy. I've seen some wonderful books for the elementary students that take a theme and have both fiction and nonfiction books on this one theme. Students have a chance to do two different types of reading, using different reading skills. They can begin to read extensively on a particular theme. Intermediate teachers also need to be wary of the appropriateness of reading materials for the age level of their students. I had a book representative exclaim to a group of teachers how a particular series on the planets and other science readings were really appropriate even for adult ESL learners because they used real photos instead of illustrations. Although the photos were "real life," the format of the books, the type size and spacing between lines cried out K–4 elementary level. They were definitely not appropriate for adults!

Another great source of reading materials for ESL students can be found on CD-ROM software. The interactive stories are wonderful. Students can hear modeled English and see the words highlighted. In some CD-ROM stories, the words are highlighted in chunks of language. Students practice reading and hearing English read in phrases instead of word by word. Broderbund's *Living Books* series has done a marvelous job of making their stories interactive and highlighting the stories in chunks of language. These stories are most appropriate for K–6 students. There are some wonderful CD-ROM software programs that have students create their own stories. One that I like in particular is called *Hollywood Theatrix* by Theatrix, Inc. Students create their own script, choose settings, and develop the characters' personalities and voices. They choose where the characters stand and move within the story. At the end, students can watch their production as if they were in a movie theater. I've used this software in my university classes where we created a class story and then watched it play out.

My last word of caution is to be careful of the "modified" reading materials out on the market. Sometimes the language has been modified so much that the reading becomes less interesting and actually more difficult to read. The beauty of the language is also lost by the "dummying down" of the text. I saw one short story that was three pages longer than the original due to the cutting of sentences to shorter ones and the adding of more explanations within the reading instead of using the easier-to-manage footnotes. The whole skill of using footnotes was lost. Because the author put everything from the original footnotes into the text itself, it became an unbearably dry piece of "literature."

14 *What is your reaction to the final paragraph above from Carolyn about "dummying down" of reading texts? Have you had similar experiences? What can you do to ensure that you use authentic texts and authentic reading tasks?*

15 *Consider the section earlier in this chapter on the use of authentic materials. Carolyn and I seem to disagree about this issue. Where do you stand on the use of authentic materials? Share your ideas with a colleague.*

16 *Think about what you have just read from Carolyn. How is her experience similar to or different from yours? What elements of her experience could benefit you? Record your ideas in your Reflective Reading Journal.*

CONCLUDING THOUGHTS

Think back to the example I used at the beginning of this chapter about my ice-skating experience. Some parallels can be drawn to planning for reading instruction and selecting appropriate reading materials. First, my interest in and excitement for ice skating made it fun. Make sure that you are interested in the materials selection and development process. Second, talk to other teachers who make the teaching of reading look so easy. What do they do to plan for reading instruction? Next, don't push yourself or your students beyond the enjoyment level too quickly. I fear that many reading teachers push their students into material beyond their ability and then the students become discouraged. When you're developing a new skill remember that you may be enjoying it, but may become tired quickly so don't push yourself. Fourth, watch your ability level. Just because there are ice skaters gliding by you with such ease and skill doesn't mean that you have to match them. Finally, the selection of appropriate reading material will come to you naturally as you continue to practice. Just as I developed a feeling of being at ease in ice skating, your ability to select appropriate materials will come to you as you practice. Take your time, make your own decisions, and be aware of what you are doing, then make the necessary adjustments so that you will continue to enjoy your teaching.

Suggested Readings

Aebersold and Field (1997) treat the topic of materials selection in two nice chapters: "Using Literature" (pp. 156–166), and "Planning the Reading Lesson" (pp. 184–197) in their book *From Reader to Reading Teacher*. Each of these chapters will provide input on factors you can consider as you determine how to select appropriate materials to meet the reading needs of the students you work with.

10

CONCLUSIONS

I have introduced to you a pedagogical framework that I have developed over several years of teaching second language reading. The framework centers around the word ACTIVE. Each letter of this word reminds me of one element for consideration in the reading classroom:

A Activate prior knowledge

C Cultivate vocabulary

T Teach for comprehension

I Increase reading rate

V Verify reading strategies

E Evaluate progress

These elements are followed by two additional considerations: the role that motivation plays in reading, and planning for and selecting appropriate reading material.

1 *Reflect back on the elements of the framework we have discussed together. Which ones stand out most in your mind? Record your ideas in your Reflective Reading Journal.*

2 *Skim through the entries in your Reflective Reading Journal. What impressions stand out in your mind as you bring these investigations to a close?*

3 *What one or two ideas that we have discussed together do you want to try out first? Discuss these with a colleague.*

One concluding thought: the pedagogical framework and ideas I have shared in this book have developed over many years of teaching ESL/EFL reading classes. I read the research on second language reading with great interest to see if what the researchers report is similar to or different from my experience in the reading classroom. I conduct research in my own reading classes to test out ideas and concepts. I encourage you to test out the issues and strategies we have addressed in this book. As you try and succeed, and more importantly, when you try and fail, make sure that you are sharing what you do with other reading teachers and documenting your own philosophy of teaching ESL/EFL readers. Keep your Reflective Reading Journal around and review it regularly as you seek to improve your skills as a teacher of reading.

4 *Skim through the entries in your Reflective Reading Journal. Take time now to write a short position paper and describe your philosophy of teaching second language reading. Share your ideas with a colleague.*

It is my hope that you have expanded your horizons and that you have thought of new ideas to apply in ESL/EFL reading classes that you will teach. I hope that you have enjoyed *Exploring Second Language Reading: Issues and Strategies.*

References

Aebersold, J. A., and M. L. Field. 1997. Planning the reading lesson. In J. A. Aebersold and M. L. Field, *From reader to reading teacher*. New York: Cambridge University Press, 184–197.

Allerson, S., and W. Grabe. 1986. Reading assessment. In F. Dubin, D. E. Eskey, and W. Grabe (eds.), *Teaching second language reading for academic purposes*. Reading, MA: Addison-Wesley Publishing Company, 161–181.

Anderson, N. J. 1991. Individual differences in strategy use in second language reading and testing. *Modern Language Journal* 75: 460–472.

Anderson, N. J. 1994. Developing ACTIVE readers: A pedagogical framework for the second language reading class. *System* 22: 177–194.

Anderson, N. J. 1996. *Real contexts*. Boston, MA: Heinle & Heinle Publishers.

Anderson, N. J. , and L. Vandergrift, 1996. Increasing metacognitive awareness in the L2 classroom by using think-aloud protocols and other verbal report formats. In R. L. Oxford, *Language Learning Strategies Around the World: Crosscultural Perspectives*. Manoa, HI: University of Hawaii Press, 3-18.

Barnett, M. 1989. *More than meets the eye: Foreign language reading*. Englewood Cliffs, NJ: Prentice Hall Regents.

Baumann, J. F. 1984. The effectiveness of a direct instruction paradigm for teaching main idea comprehension. *Reading Research Quarterly* 20: 93–115.

Betts, E. A. 1957. *Foundations of reading instruction*. New York: American Book Company

Brown, A. L., A. S. Palinscar, and B. B. Armbruster. 1984. Instructing comprehension-fostering activities in interactive learning situations. In H. Mandl, N. L. Stein, and T. Trabasso (eds.), *Learning and comprehension of text*. Hillsdale, NJ: Lawrence Erlbaum, 255–286.

Caine, R. N., and G. Caine. 1997. *Unleashing the power of perceptual change: The potential of brain-based teaching*. Alexandria, VA: Association for Supervision and Curriculum Development.

Carpenter, P., and M. Just. 1986. Cognitive processes in reading. In J. Orasanu (ed.), *Reading comprehension: From theory to practice*. Hillsdale, N. J.: Lawrence Erlbaum, 11–29.

Carrell, P. L. 1983a. Background knowledge in second language comprehension. *Language Learning and Communication* 2: 25–34.

Carrell, P. L. 1983b. Some issues in studying the role of schemata, or background knowledge, in second language comprehension. *Reading in a Foreign Language* 1: 81–92.

Carrell, P.L. 1984. The effects of rhetorical organization on ESL readers. *TESOL Quarterly* 18: 441–469.

Carrell, P. L. 1985. Facilitating ESL reading by teaching text structure.
TESOL Quarterly 19: 727–752.

Carrell, P. L., and J. C. Eisterhold. 1983. Schema theory and ESL reading pedagogy.
TESOL Quarterly 17: 553–573.

Carrell, P. L., B. G. Pharis, and J. C. Liberto. 1989. Metacognitive strategy training
for ESL reading. *TESOL Quarterly* 23: 647–678.

Carrell, P. L., and U. Connor. 1991, March. Reading and writing different genres.
Paper presented at the Twenty-fifth annual conference of Teachers of English to
Speakers of Other Languages, New York.

Carver, R. P. 1990. *Reading rate: A review of research and theory.*
San Diego: Academic Press.

Chamot, A. U., and J. M. O'Malley. 1994. *The CALLA handbook.* Reading, MA:
Addison-Wesley Publishing Company.

Christison, M. A. 1997. Applying mind-brain principles to L2 teaching.
TESOL Matters 7 (4): 3.

Coady, J., J. Magoto, P. Hubbard, J. Graney, and K. Mokhtari. 1993. High frequency
vocabulary and reading proficiency in ESL reading. In T. Huckin, M. Haynes,
and J. Coady (eds.), *Second language reading and vocabulary learning.*
Norwood, NJ: Ablex, 217–28.

Cohen, A. D. 1987. The use of verbal and imagery mnemonics in second-language
vocabulary learning. *Studies in Second Language Acquisition* 9: 43–62.

Cohen, A. D. 1990. *Language learning: Insights for learners, teachers, and researchers.*
New York: Newbury House.

Crookes, G., and R. Schmidt. 1991. Motivation: Reopening the research agenda.
Language Learning 41: 469–512.

Cushing Weigle, S., and L. Jensen. 1996. Reading rate improvement in university ESL
classes. *The CATESOL Journal* 9: 55–71.

Davey, E. 1983. Think aloud—Modeling the cognitive processes of reading
comprehension. *Journal of Reading* 27: 44–47.

Day, R. R., and J. Bamford. 1998. *Extensive reading in the second language classroom.*
New York: Cambridge University Press.

Dörnyei, Z. 1994a. Motivation and motivating in the foreign language classroom.
Modern Language Journal 78: 273–284.

Dörnyei, Z. 1994b. Understanding L2 motivation: On with the challenge!
Modern Language Journal 78: 515–523.

Dubin, F., and D. Bycina. 1991. Academic reading and the ESL/EFL teacher.
In M. Celce-Murcia (ed.), *Teaching English as a second or foreign language*
(2nd ed.). New York: Newbury House, 195–215.

Dulin, K. L. 1978. Reading and the affective domain. In S. Pflaum-Connor (ed.),
Aspects of reading education. Berkeley, CA: McCutcheon Publishing, 106–125.

Ericsson, K. A., and H. A. Simon. 1984. *Protocol analysis: Verbal reports as data.*
Cambridge, MA: The MIT Press.

Eskey, D. E. 1986. Theoretical foundations. In F. Dubin, D. E. Eskey, and W. Grabe
(eds.), *Teaching second language reading for academic purposes.* Reading, MA:
Addison-Wesley Publishing Company, 3–23.

Freeman, D., and Y. Freeman. 1992. Is whole language teaching compatible with content-based instruction? *CATESOL Journal 5*: 103–108.

Fry, E. B. 1975. *Reading drills for speed and comprehension* (2nd ed.). Providence, RI: Jamestown Publishers.

Gardner, R. C., and W. E. Lambert. 1982. Language attitudes and language learning. In E. B. Ryan and H. Giles (eds.), *Attitudes towards language variation*. London: Arnold, 132–147.

Garner, R. 1982. Verbal-report data on reading strategies. *Journal of Reading Behavior 14*: 159–167.

Garner, R., G. B. Macready, and S. Wagoner. 1984. Reader's acquisition of the components of the text-lookback strategy. *Journal of Educational Psychology 76*: 300–309.

Goodman, K. S. 1973. Psycholinguistic universals of the reading process. In F. Smith (ed.), *Psycholinguistics and reading*. New York: Holt, Rinehart, and Winston, 177–182.

Goodman, K. S. 1976. Reading: A psycholinguistic guessing game. In H. Singer and R. B. Ruddell (eds.), *Theoretical Models and Processes of Reading* (2nd ed.). Newark, DE: International Reading Association, 497–508.

Gough, P. B. 1985. One second of reading. In H. Singer and R. B. Ruddell (eds.), *Theoretical Models and Processes of Reading* (3rd ed.). Newark, DE: International Reading Association, 661–686.

Grabe, W. 1991. Current developments in second language reading research. *TESOL Quarterly 25*: 375–406.

Grabe, W. 1997. Discourse analysis and reading instruction. In T. Miller (ed.), *Functional approaches to written text: Classroom applications*. Washington, DC: United States Information Agency, 2–15.

Harrison, C. 1992. The reading process and learning to read. In C. Harrison and M. Coles (eds.), *The reading for real handbook*. London: Routledge, 3–28.

Harris, D. P. 1966. *Reading improvement exercises for students of English as a second language*. Englewood Cliffs, NJ: Prentice-Hall, Inc.

Hatch, E., and C. Brown. 1995. *Vocabulary, semantics, and language education*. New York: Cambridge University Press.

Heimlich, J. E., and S. D. Pittelman. 1986. *Semantic mapping: Classroom applications*. Newark, DE: International Reading Association.

Higgins, J., and R. Wallace. 1989. Hopalong: A computer reader pacer. *System 17*: 389–399.

Huckin, T., M. Haynes, and J. Coady. 1993. *Second language reading and vocabulary learning*. Norwood, NJ: Ablex.

Irwin, J. W. 1991. *Teaching reading comprehension processes* (2nd ed.). Englewood Cliffs, NJ: Prentice Hall.

Irwin, J. W., and I. Baker. 1989. *Promoting active reading comprehension strategies: A resource book for teachers*. Englewood Cliffs, NJ: Prentice Hall.

Jensen, L. 1986. Advanced reading skills in a comprehensive course. In F. Dubin, D. E. Eskey, and W. Grabe (eds.), *Teaching second language reading for academic purposes*. Reading, MA: Addison-Wesley Publishing Company, 103–124.

Kern, R. 1989. Second language reading strategy instruction: Its effects on comprehension and word inference ability. *Modern Language Journal* 73: 135–149.

Levine, A., and T. Reves. 1990. Does the method of vocabulary presentation make a difference? *TESL Canada Journal* 8: 37–51.

MacLean, M., and A. d'Anglejan. 1986. Rational cloze and retrospection: Insights into first and second language reading comprehension. *The Canadian Modern Language Review* 42: 814–826.

Maclin, A. 1996. *Reference guide to English: A handbook of English as a second language.* Washington, DC: United States Information Agency.

McNeil, J. D. 1987. *Reading comprehension: New directions for classroom practice* (2nd ed.). Glenview, IL: Scott, Foresman & Company.

Murtagh, L. 1989. Reading in a second or foreign language: models, processes, and pedagogy. *Language, Culture and Curriculum* 2: 91–105.

Nation, I. S. P. 1990. *Teaching and learning vocabulary.* New York: Newbury House.

Nation, I. S. P., and J. Magoto (n.d.). *The university word list: Vocabulary for students preparing to do academic study.* Unpublished manuscript, Ohio University, Athens, Ohio.

Nuttall, C. 1982. *Teaching reading skills in a foreign language.* Oxford: Heinemann.

Nuttall, C. 1996. *Teaching reading skills in a foreign language* (new edition). Oxford: Heinemann.

O'Malley, J. M., and L. Valdez-Pierce. 1996. *Authentic assessment for English language learners.* White Plains, NY: Addison-Wesley Publishing Company.

Oxford, R. L. 1990. *Language learning strategies: What every teacher should know.* New York: Newbury House Publishers.

Palincsar, A. S., and A. L. Brown. 1984. Reciprocal teaching of comprehension fostering and comprehension activities. *Cognition and Instruction* 1: 117–175.

Peregoy, S. F., and O. F. Boyle. 1997. *Reading, writing, and learning in ESL.* New York: Longman Publishers.

Perkins, D. 1995. *Outsmarting IQ: The emerging science of learnable intelligence.* New York: The Free Press.

Plaister, T. 1968. Reading instruction for college foreign students. *TESOL Quarterly* 2: 164–169.

Pressley, M., J. R. Levin, and G. E. Miller. 1982. The keyword method compared to alternative vocabulary learning strategies. *Contemporary Educational Psychology* 7: 50–60.

Pritchard, R. 1990. The effects of cultural schemata on reading processing strategies. *Reading Research Quarterly* 25: 273–295.

Rayner, K., and A. Pollatsek. 1989. *The psychology of reading.* Englewood Cliffs, N. J.: Prentice Hall.

Reid, J. (ed.). 1995. *Learning styles in the ESL/EFL classroom.* Boston, MA: Heinle & Heinle Publishers.

Richard-Amato, P. A. 1996. *Making it happen: Interaction in the second language classroom.* White Plains, NY: Longman Publishers.

Riley, P. M. 1975. Improving reading comprehension. In A. Newton (ed.), *The art of TESOL, Part II.* Washington, DC: English Teaching Forum, 198–200.

Robinson, H. A., V. Faraone, D. R. Hittleman, and E. Unruh. 1990. *Reading comprehension instruction 1783–1987: A review of trends and research.* Newark, DE: International Reading Association.

Rumelhart, D. E. 1985. Toward an interactive model of reading. In H. Singer and R. B. Ruddell (eds.), *Theoretical models and processes of reading* (3rd ed.). Newark, DE: International Reading Association, 722–750.

Samuels, S. J. 1979. The method of repeated readings. *The Reading Teacher,* 32: 403–408.

Savage, K. L. 1992. Lesson Planning. In *Teacher training through video.* New York: Longman Publishing Group.

Scarcella, R., and R. L. Oxford. 1992. *The tapestry of language learning: The individual in the communicative classroom.* Boston, MA: Heinle & Heinle Publishers.

Segalowitz, N., C. Poulsen, and M. Komoda. 1991. Lower level components of reading skill in higher level bilinguals: Implications for reading instruction. *AILA Review* 8: 15–30.

Seliger, H. W. 1972. Improving reading speed and comprehension in English as a second language. *English Language Teaching* 27: 48–55.

Snow, M. A. (ed.) 1994. *Project LEAP: Learning English-for-academic-purposes, training manual—year three.* Los Angeles: California State University, Los Angeles.

Spargo, E., and G. R. Williston. 1980. *Timed readings books 1–10.* Providence, RI: Jamestown Publishers, Inc.

Stanovich, K. E. 1980. Toward an interactive-compensatory model of individual differences in the development of reading fluency. *Reading Research Quarterly* 16: 32–71.

Stoller, F. 1986. Reading lab: Developing low-level reading skills. In F. Dubin, D. E. Eskey, and W. Grabe (eds.), *Teaching second language reading for academic purposes.* Reading, MA: Addison-Wesley Publishing Company, 51–76.

Stoller, F. L., and W. Grabe. 1997. A six T's approach to content-based instruction. In M. A. Snow and D. M. Brinton (eds.), *The content-based classroom: Perspectives on integrating language and content.* White Plains, NY: Longman, 78–94.

Swaffar, J., K. Arens, and H. Byrnes. 1991. *Reading for meaning: An integrated approach to language learning.* Englewood Cliffs, NJ: Prentice Hall.

Teachers of English to Speakers of Other Languages, Inc. 1997. *ESL standards for pre-K–12 students.* Alexandria, VA: Teachers of English to Speakers of Other Languages.

Wallace, C. 1992. *Reading.* New York: Oxford University Press.

Weber, R. 1991. Linguistic diversity and reading in an American society. In R. Barr, P. Kamil, P. Mosenthal, and D. P. Pearson (eds.), *Handbook of reading research* (vol. 2). New York: Longman, 97–119.

Winograd, P., and V. C. Hare. 1988. Direct instruction of reading comprehension strategies: The nature of teacher explanation. In C. E. Weinstein, E. T. Goetz, and P. A. Alexander, P. A. (eds.), *Learning and study strategies: Issues in assessment, instruction, and evaluation.* San Diego, CA: Academic Press, Inc., 121–139.

Zhang, W. 1995. A study on Chinese secondary school EFL students' strategy use and motivation for language learning. Unpublished doctoral dissertation, Ohio University, Athens, Ohio.